Praise for *Selling fr*

In *Selling from the Heart*, Larry myths about how to approach buyers and close the sale shows you how, in a world suffering from information overload and technology fatigue, sales professionals who demonstrate authenticity and empathy gain an unbeatable competitive edge.

-Jeb Blount, CEO SalesGravy.com and author of *Sales EQ*

Too many of us (salespeople) look outward for success and in the most brilliant, down to earth way, *Selling from the Heart* reminds us that our success starts within, not out. In a world of copy cats, Larry Levine, with a softness of a benevolent mentor and the disarming approach of Fred Rogers, stresses that we can't win as a copy, but only as an original. "Be YOU!" The best message the sales world has received in a long time.

-Keenan, CEO of A Sales Guy

Selling from the Heart is not really a book about sales. It's a book about YOU. This is the ultimate playbook for showing up as yourself, so you can increase your sales.

-Deb Calvert, author of *DISCOVER Questions*®
and co-author of *Stop Selling & Start Leading*

Selling from the Heart is a masterpiece of authenticity. Larry Levine articulates how intention matters more than technique, and if you sell with genuine purpose revenue will follow. Great sales professionals focus on the value they bring to customers, not just the value they will receive. I recommend this book to every salesperson. Not only will this book make you successful, but it also makes selling even more enjoyable.

-James Muir, CEO, Best Practice International
and author of *The Perfect Close*

Real sales, real world, real life. Larry Levine shares what it takes to be an authentically successful salesperson. *Selling from the Heart* will have you probing your own heart, and when you read and apply the lessons from the book, you'll find yourself seeing authentically.

-**Mark Hunter,** CSP, "The Sales Hunter" author of
High-Profit Prospecting and *High-Profit Selling*

Selling from the Heart is powerful, refreshing, and . . . authentic! Larry Levine and this new book are a breath of much-needed fresh air. He's the most honest social selling expert in the business, and this book is exactly what sellers need today. Larry shares wisdom from his years of successful experience, with both blunt truth and effective advice. You will love his writing style, stories, and most of all, the increased sales from implementing his advice!

-**Mike Weinberg,** author of *New Sales Simplified*
and *Sales Management Simplified*

In sales, the heart always comes before the head. What I love and admire most about Larry Levine is that he sees the potential in all of us and compels us to act with heart and authenticity. In *Selling from the Heart*, Larry draws upon the wisdom that is both timeless and relevant. Read it and increase your sales, but more importantly, connect with yourself and live a more meaningful life.

-**Shari Levitin,** founder and CEO of Levitin Group
and author of *Heart and Sell-10 Universal T*
ruths Every Salesperson Needs to Know

Selling from the Heart

In *Selling from the Heart*, you are going to find many of the keys to success in sales. You're going to learn to embrace who you are and to do the hard work that always results in success and results. More importantly, you are going to learn to sell from the heart, care and be the killer app in sales. If you want to learn how to improve your sales, the best place to start is from someone who has successfully sold what others perceive to be a commodity. Larry Levine's book is worth your time, your attention, and should be applied with a great sense of urgency.

-**Anthony Iannarino,** author of *Eat Their Lunch: Winning Customers Away from Your Competitors*

Larry holds a window up to every salesperson and questions, "Why do you do what you do?" This process of self-reflection helps the reader distill their mindset to a time-tested, winning sales formula: adopt a customer-centric approach and never compromise upon your integrity. This is *Selling from the Heart* and the secret sauce that fuels the very best salespeople.

-**Lee Bartlett,** author of *The No.1 Best Seller*

Larry's approach to his new book is like he says, "from the heart." This is a no B.S. approach to selling in the new millennium, it may even hurt to hear the truth on the change that you need to be! Too often Business Books can be regimented or produced to a "cookie cutter" formula. Larry Levine, in *Selling from the Heart* has written from the heart, stacked with experience and case study anecdotes from his twenty-seven-year successful sales career.

-**Tim Hughes,** CEO and co-founder of Digital Leadership Associates, www.social-experts.net

Larry Levine's *Selling from the Heart* is a spirited view into a superior salesperson's brain. Customer centric self-awareness is a rare quality found only the most gifted of sales professionals, but this gift can be learned. Learn to Sell From The Heart! Buy this book today!

-**Patrick Tinney,** author of *Unlocking Yes* and *Perpetual Hunger*

Selling from the Heart should be mandatory reading for everyone in a sales role. With poignant stories and observations matched with expert insights and actions, you'll want to dive into this book sooner than later. It will help you differentiate yourself in a sea of same sellers and show you that "selling from the heart" will soon be the only way a sales professional can serve their client's needs and crush their quota at the same time.

-**Phil Gerbyshak,** digital selling strategist and sales trainer

Success in sales starts with a commitment to YOU and holding yourself to the highest professional standards. Too many reps today find excuses for their failure too quickly in today's world of, "anything except face-to-face meetings," and the rise of, "the silent sales floor." Larry lays out a great methodology to self-reflect on the trajectory of your sales career and either turn it around or supercharge it for the future. Having built a personal relationship with Larry myself and learning about his personal story over the years, I would highly recommend this book to any seller at any stage of their career.

-**Brian Signorelli,** sales director, HubSpot, Inc.

Selling from the Heart succinctly describes what it takes to be an authentic salesperson. It's a fast-paced narrative that grabs you emotionally from the first page and never let go. For newbies to sales it's a primer for happiness and prosperity. For successful sales reps it's a refreshing reminder that genuinely caring about your customers and the value you provide is the secret sauce. For those struggling in sales it's a pathway to improvement.

-Tom Williams, managing director Strategic Dynamics Inc. and co-author of *The Seller's Challenge: How Top Sellers Master 10 Deal Killing Obstacles in B2B Sales*

What Larry's Clients Have To Say

They say that actions speak louder than words, so when Larry asked me to write a personal character reference for this book, I knew I had to take action. You see that is what Larry does—he inspires action. I have seen this first hand at a partner conference where he took a room full of seasoned (read skeptical) copier business owners from, "Social media has no place in my business," to "I need to get back and maximize how my sales reps are using social media"—it's a sight to behold. If you engage in any kind of social media activity with Larry, whether LinkedIn or Twitter, you can rely on him to reply with a thoughtful response—he really does walk the talk, every single day. If I were to sum up my personal experience of Larry, I would say he is authentic, genuine, and one of the few people who has cracked the social selling code.

-Andy Hill, head of Digitally Mastery, Xerox

Larry Levine is a true and authentic sales leader. There are not many sales professionals that have made the transition from the analog style of selling to embracing social. More importantly, Larry talks the talk and walks the walk. Everything Larry says and does is from a practicality point of view. It works, it makes sense and most importantly he speaks from the heart.

-Hari Tharmakumar, national channel manager,
Toshiba Australia

Sales is the same as it ever was, but buyers have changed because of technology. Today's buyer requires authentic salespeople that can bring value beyond their product or service and there is no one more authentic than my friend Larry Levine. Larry is deeply invested in speaking the truth and I have been blessed to have him mentor me in my pursuit of learning how to adapt my sales system for today's Social World. His new book, *Selling from the Heart*, is an opportunity for many more of you to begin a relationship with Larry and take your sales to the next level while maintaining and enhancing what makes your expression of humanity unique and special. Enjoy the ride!

-**Mike Garrison,** Garrison Sales Consulting

Larry Levine is excellent at what he does! He's an enthusiastic presenter, innovative thinker and thought-provoking writer. I have been blessed to have met Larry several years ago and to learn from him since then. Larry has been working with our sales team and it has improved our digital presence in the marketplace, expanded our reach & connections and led to new sales. I encourage everyone in business-to-business sales or in a marketing role to read *Selling from the Heart* and learn valuable lessons to improve your brand and increase your performance!

-**Joshua Justice,** President, JustTech

A refreshing outlook outside of traditional sales books and trainings. Larry Levine enables you with the right tools to dig deep and find the real YOU! *Selling from the Heart* will make you feel empowered and ready to develop your OWN road map of success personally and professionally. The only drawback is how long do I have to wait for the sequel? Five Stars! I had the pleasure of hearing Larry Levine speak a few years ago. I knew as a sales rep, I was different and unique. I truly cared about my clients and relationships. I was unsure and lacked confidence on how to communicate this effectively in the marketplace. After Larry's presentation, I did my homework. I can tell you it was at this moment I shifted from a "sales rep" to a "sales professional." By taking the time to understand my client's needs, what value I brought to the table, I was able to really communicate my brand. Larry Levine is an amazing mentor. I keep fine tuning my story and brand. Not necessarily because my sales have gone stale, but because Larry has helped me see the true value that I can personally bring by always being at my best for my clients. In the sales world, I've been told, "You care too much. Don't spend so much time on that issue, go get the next sale!" Larry has provided me with the confidence to be my true authentic self. As a professional, I know I'm making a difference. Thank you, Larry for your continued support and keeping it real. I have not only benefited from your training, but my clients and partnerships have seen the return too!

-**Carrie McCann,** account manager, ProvenIT

No more old techniques or lies that don't work, this is the new "how to manual" for any sales manager wanting to improve their sales team, or any salesperson wanting to get better.

-**Andrew Jones,** national sales operations manager, Australia Electronic Imaging Division, Toshiba (Australia) Pty Limited

SELLING
— from the —
HEART

How Your
Authentic Self
Sells You!

LARRY LEVINE

NEW YORK

LONDON • NASHVILLE • MELBOURNE • VANCOUVER

SELLING FROM THE HEART

How Your Authentic Self Sells You

Published in New York, New York, by Morgan James Publishing. Morgan James is a trademark of Morgan James, LLC. www.MorganJamesPublishing.com

Scripture taken from THE HOLY BIBLE, NEW INTERNATIONAL VERSION®. Copyright©1973, 1978, 1984, 2011 by Biblica, Inc.™. Used by permission of Zondervan

Proudly distributed by Publishers Group West®

A **FREE** ebook edition is available for you or a friend with the purchase of this print book.

CLEARLY SIGN YOUR NAME ABOVE

Instructions to claim your free ebook edition:
1. Visit MorganJamesBOGO.com
2. Sign your name CLEARLY in the space above
3. Complete the form and submit a photo of this entire page
4. You or your friend can download the ebook to your preferred device

ISBN 9781636981741 paperback
ISBN 9781636981758 ebook
Library of Congress Control Number: 2023934031

Cover Design by:
Jeremy B Clark
jeremybclark.com

Interior Design by:
Chris Treccani
www.3dogcreative.net

Morgan James is a proud partner of Habitat for Humanity Peninsula and Greater Williamsburg. Partners in building since 2006.

Get involved today! Visit: www.morgan-james-publishing.com/giving-back

To my loving and supportive wife, Robin . . .
You've always supported my grit, grind, and grow philosophy in life.
You're my rock, my shoulder, my strength, my all, and my everything.
I don't know how I could have done this without you. Thank you for
being there when I needed you the most. You've been there every
step of the way. All I can say is, "We did it!"

Table of Contents

Acknowledgments

Over twenty years ago, I made a promise to myself and more importantly to my wife that I would write my first book by the time I was fifty years old. Well, sometimes in life, "you know what" happens, but at fifty-three, I'm proud to say, "Babe, I've done it".

Life is so unpredictable. I can only think back to the 1994 *Forrest Gump* movie and the famous line by Tom Hanks, "My mom always said life is like a box of chocolates. You never know what you're going to get."

In 2015, my box of chocolates happened and instead of saying to myself, "You never know what you're going to get (may I add 'dealt')," I did something about it.

With the encouragement of my wife and my close friend Darrell Amy, I set out to charter a new chapter in my life. I remember the conversation with Darrell back in 2015, "You've accomplished so much in your sales career, it's time you share you with the sales world." I'm forever grateful to you Darrell for the support, the friendship, the listening, the many road trips together and more importantly, our partnership. The *Selling from the Heart* podcast as well as the Social Sales Academy has become the foundation of who we are genuine, authentic, two real guys who speak from the heart!

I'll never forget the summer of 2017 road trip to Austin, Texas, as you held me hostage in your car convincing me why I should write a book. In writing *Selling from the Heart*, I found me. I found my inner voice and why self-alignment is mission critical to those in sales. Without a beating heart, life becomes lifeless. Without your heart and mind in your career, one becomes lifeless.

To Keenan, I remember my first conversation with you, December of 2015. You didn't have to, but you spent the time with me. You listened to me, sharing your story and advice. With your encouragement, I remember committing on that call that I would write every week. I haven't stopped since . . . You inspired me to share my story in ways I never could have dreamed of, thank you!

A heartfelt thank you to Bernadette McClelland. We met through comments on a blog post, and instantaneously we hit it off. You are a true kindred spirit. I can't thank you enough for the countless hours of listening and advice you've given me. A real highlight for me was my trip to Melbourne, Australia. You and your family are so very special to me; Tim, Danielle, and Matt are amazing. You will forever be a part of my life. Friendship bridges continents when you speak from the heart.

To my personal board of directors . . . Darrell Amy, Scott MacGregor, and Mike Garrison. You know my story. You've been right there by my side. You've kept me in line, you've listened, you've been mentors and coaches to me. I love you guys!

I often refer to sales as "the art of the give and the art of the help." To all the members of the Kiwanis Club of Thousand Oaks, you've taught me why giving is so important because to get, one must be willing to give. You taught me what it means to give back. This is why I enjoy leading with my heart.

A servant's mindset is at the forefront of a *Selling from the Heart* professional. One becomes a servant by learning how to give of oneself.

A special thank you to the following four guys: Jeb Blount, Anthony Iannarino, Mike Weinberg and Mark Hunter. You believed enough in me to invite me to Outbound 2018.

To James Muir, Shari Levitin, Patrick Tinney, Phil Gerbyshak, Tim Hughes and Brian Signorelli: your support has been overwhelming. You are all true *Selling from the Heart* champions.

To the one and only, Lee Bartlett: from across the pond, you've been there to listen consistently and cheer me on. You truly represent what it means to be authentic, the real deal and speak from the heart!

Thanks to Kim Thompson-Pinder and her team from RTI Publishing. They were great to work with, and their collaboration and support made this book possible. And to David Hancock and his team at Morgan James Publishing who brought the book back to life and redistributed it around the world.

To my loving and supportive wife, Robin: you've been there every step of the way. You've listened, you've been a shoulder to lean on (sometimes to cry on) and my rock during the countless hours I spent writing this book.

Inside *Selling from the Heart*, I poured my love for sales into every page. Please take this book to heart and place yourself and your career upon a business pedestal. You deserve it, and your career deserves the best version of YOU.

I hope you enjoy *Selling from the Heart*.

Forewords

I t is amazing how people can get connected these days. It started with a LinkedIn post. From there it progressed to a Skype call. Not long afterward, he took me to dinner—with our respective partners of course! And then he read, and reread, *my* book and hey, presto! I have now been given the privilege of writing the foreword for *his* book. My friend, Larry Levine— *Selling from the Heart*!

Many people in the world of sales will negate the power of building a friendship in business. They will negate the power behind social relationships. But building a relationship and forging a friendship are very different beasts. Or are they?

In many cases, it is true that our buyers aren't there to build friendships. They are there to do business and at the heart of every business is a relationship of sorts. And that is what we, as sellers, need to include in our strategic planning: identifying the heart of a business and the heart of a business relationship.

Done well, you may also build a friendship and if you do— consider yourself extremely fortunate!

Business today, in many instances, is lacking something. We have all the resources available to us—the technology and the tools, and we are well aware of all the new trends surrounding our business and our prospects, but what seems to be missing is the genuine relationships—that make a business connection authentic.

The result is the inability of many to build quality pipelines based on understanding the real needs of a prospective client.

Selling from the Heart has a focus on bringing the authentic you to the sales table that allows you not just to build those much-needed relationships but have the commercial conversations that lead to increased business success. Larry Levine has captured that concept so well in the pages that follow.

Being able to differentiate between a sales rep and a sales professional may not be a big deal to a salesperson, but you will find out why it is such a big deal to a buyer, and our buyers today are looking for those salespeople they can trust—those salespeople who are comfortable being themselves.

Sales leaders are also looking for salespeople they can trust to run their businesses—how can you do that if you don't have the self-awareness with which to leverage your growth, let alone your prospects and customers?

The focus of sales performance is shifting more and more from the techniques and hard skills to the soft skills that matter. Self-awareness is one of those skills.

Larry Levine shares insights in this book on how self-awareness leads you to create an authentic brand for yourself in the marketplace. This is the era of people buying from people they know, like and trust more than ever, and this book addresses not just the why, but the how as well.

He is able to do this because he walks his talk. He has done this in the corporate world and now he practices what he preaches in his own business.

Whether you are a rookie wanting to prospect, whether you are a veteran wanting to know how to brand yourself or whether you are someone in between wanting to know how to write content in this rapidly changing business environment, this book has all of that—and more . . .

Given that you are reading this foreword, then you have committed to reading the remainder of the book, committed to being the best version of you in order to stand head and shoulders above the rest, committed enough to not fight over the crumbs of the sales environment, but play for a bigger slice of the pie, that is yours for the giving and taking.

It's time now to lift the bar even more.

-**Bernadette McClelland**, CEO of 3 Red Folders,
Australia author, *The Art of Commercial Conversations:
When It's Your Turn To Make A Difference*

———————

Fourteen years ago, I was wrapping up a training session on solution selling strategies at an industry trade show when Larry Levine first walked into my life. While other tenured reps were digging in their heels, complaining about the need to change their sales approach, Larry was the exact opposite. He wanted to know what he could do to integrate the ideas I had just shared into his process.

Over the years, we continued to stay in touch. I watched Larry stay on the cutting edge, always looking for new ways to grow as a professional. I watched him hire a professional branding consultant to build a website that he used to share ideas with his prospects. When LinkedIn came onto the scene, he devoured the platform, once again eager to embrace new ideas to grow.

In April 2016, Larry and I were delivering a training session at an event in Las Vegas. True to his spirit of being an innovator and wanting to add value, Larry suggested that we start a podcast. In reply, I said that it sounded like fun and asked him what we should call it. Without hesitating, he said, "Let's call it *Selling From the Heart*."

That began a journey that has introduced us to a community of amazing sales professionals from all over the world that feel the same way we do: it's time to bring the heart back into the sales profession!

Spend a few minutes with Larry, and you discover a true professional, passionate about improving himself and helping others. It's this contagious attitude that you'll find woven throughout the pages of *Selling from the Heart*.

Every one of your competitors has access to similar sales tools and tactics. Most likely there isn't a whole lot of difference between your products or services and your competition.

In this environment, how are you going to win? You need to do something different.

At first glance, it may seem that the idea of *Selling from the Heart* is a little "touchy-feely" and not focused on results. However, I've come to agree with Larry that the true "x-factor" that differentiates the winners is that they are genuine, and they give a rip about their clients' success. They want to help. They don't need a sales manager to push them. They are driven to succeed and willing to work hard to earn a great living.

When you sell from the heart, you introduce a whole new dynamic into the sales process that creates powerful differentiation. That helps you win more deals which is not touchy-feely at all. But it also does something else: In addition to making more sales, you get to make a difference. *Selling from the Heart* equals more money plus more meaning.

As I watch Larry coach high-performance reps and teams, I get a front row seat to see how his belief of *Selling from the Heart* makes a difference in the lives of sales reps. Yes, reps are growing their income. But more than that, I'm seeing them come alive with a new sense of purpose. That's a double win that is truly a game changer.

In this book, you'll discover the same things I have when spending time with Larry. You'll be inspired as he leads you to discover new sources of passion for what you do. You'll also be instructed in very practical ways how you can enhance the value you bring to your clients and thus the compensation you get in return.

As I've come to be good friends with Larry, I've become a better professional and a better person. I truly believe that as you enjoy the pages of this book, you will as well.

As I read this book, I found myself taking a lot of notes and even journaling. I encourage you to do the same. Take these words as the advice of a coach and incorporate them into your professional and personal life. You're going to love how it feels to sell from the heart!

-**Darrell Amy**, co-host of the *Selling from the Heart* Podcast
and author of *Revenue Growth Engine*

Introduction

Authenticity. This was the word that started me on the journey of *Selling from the Heart*. As I watched how the sales world used "all about me" and manipulative tactics, I knew that something had to change, and it had to start with me.

Who was I? That question burned inside of me. It consumed every bit of me. I had to take a good long look inside myself. Was I authentic? Was I leading an authentic lifestyle? The answer was "Yes." Did I have more to learn about myself on this excursion? The answer was also "Yes." I could honestly say that I was giving and bringing the best of myself, but yearned for more.

With that settled, where was I to begin? I knew that this message was going to rock the sales world. For too many unfortunate years, "sales" was a four-letter word because of the actions of salespeople and the leadership that turn a blind eye to what was really going on. Now, it was time for that to change.

I started the *Selling from the Heart* Podcast with my close and dear friend Darrell Amy as a way of getting the message out there. On LinkedIn, I looked for other sales leaders and sales-people who felt the same way I did and made close connections with them. Many articles were written and posted to help explain what being authentic meant in sales, and guess what? People began to get it.

The time came when I knew I had to go bigger, and that is when the idea for this book was born. I thought I knew what it meant to be authentic, but now I was going to have to put my money where my mouth was.

Writing this book helped clarify what my right message was and how it had to be delivered. I'm a huge advocate and believer that words matter and so does the message.

To be honest, at first, I figured it would help me get on a few stages, and if I sold a few books and helped a few people, I would have been happy. Little did I know how viral this was going to go and how many lives it was going to change. It did not only go to the International Best-Seller list, but at the time of this writing, it has well over one hundred five-star reviews on Amazon.

Fast forward to the challenging, uncertain, and turbulent times that have rocked the sales industry since 2020 and the core principles around *Selling from the Heart* have become the saving grace and mainstay for many around the world.

I pinch myself every day. For some, it would puff them up, but for me, I am honored beyond words that others have allowed my writing to make a difference in their life. Just recently, I redid the original introduction, which you are reading now. I wanted to thank the people who have not only embraced this message, but shared it. There are so many that I could never list them all, but if you are reading this revised introduction, then you know who you are, and I am grateful.

If you would like to gain an understanding of the impact the book has had, then head on over to www.sellingfromtheheart.net.

This book is divided into two sections: **Finding Your Authentic You** and **The Sales Skills of an Authentic Sales Professional**. Why not start with the skills first? Success always comes from the inside out. If you are not true to yourself, then how can you be true to others?

Authenticity is the key to being a sales professional instead of a sales rep. Authenticity is a lifestyle, not a light switch. When you know who you are, then there is a confidence that shines through in all that you do and allows you to be of service to others without expecting anything in return.

Authenticity allows you to get rid of sales chaos, where you must be in control of everything. You recognize your strengths, embrace your weaknesses, and can enable others to help you in areas where you are not strong. Another amazing thing is that you no longer have an excuse for not doing what you know you should be doing.

When you are truly yourself, you learn to own your story and use it to sell. It becomes a strong connection tool to create lasting relationships and share concepts in a powerful way.

Lastly, is your mindset. What goes on in the three pounds of grey matter between your ears is what determines whether you don't make your quota, just make your quota, or exceed it.

In the second section, we get to your skills. Now, you have to put into practice what you believe in your heart. Goals are reached when consistent action is taken. It's all about the non-negotiables.

What is the most essential action to take? Prospecting. If you want to have an ever-flowing sales funnel, then you must develop an ever-flowing relationship funnel. It's the daily commitment you make to yourself to open up new conversations, new connections, and new relationships.

Next is leadership. If you want to sell from the heart, you must learn and commit to servant-leadership. Without it, your ego takes over, and you start to look at your clients through dollar-signed glasses.

Selling is not complete once you obtain a signature on the dotted line. Your current clients are vital to your sales growth, and if you take care of them, they will stay with you for life. At the core of your sales skills is communication; without it, you are sunk. You must give a rip about your clients if you want them to give a rip about you.

Spoiler Alert: Whoever thought that an empty suit would come to mean so much to so many? (Read Chapter 10). The first time I brought one on stage, it became an instant hit and I now travel with at least two of them when I go to speak at events.

Are you ready to change not only your life, but the life of your family, clients, and your community? Sales success has its perks, and two of them are that you can be generous with your money and your time to make other's lives better. This, my friends, is what a servant-led sales professional is all about.

I encourage you to turn the page and start your journey to becoming a true sales professional.

I encourage you to download the self-reflection journal at www.sellingfromtheheart.net/journal, as this reinforces each chapter and helps you to uncover the authentic sales professional that I know you can become.

Section 1:

Finding Your Authentic You

Chapter 1

I Finally Found the Real Me

"People don't buy what you do, they buy why you do it.
And what you do simply proves what you believe."
Simon Sinek, *Start with Why: How Great Leaders*
Inspire Everyone to Take Action

Would you be shocked if I told you my sales career started with drugs? No, I wasn't a drug dealer hanging out on a street corner, trying to sell without getting caught. Throughout high school, I worked in a pharmacy. I started out delivering prescription medicine to the elderly. This is where I got my first taste of what it meant to develop genuine, authentic and real relationships. It made my day to be able to help the elderly by delivering to them what they needed. The 'relationship bug' bit me and I loved it!

As time progressed, I received a promotion to a pharmacy tech position. I loved watching all the pharmaceutical sales reps come in, sporting their fancy suits. I would observe their interactions and how well they were developing relationships with the pharmacist. I became fascinated or, should I say, obsessed with the lifestyle of a pharmacist, and I figured, "What the heck. I'm going to become a pharmacist." No, I am not joking.

I thought I had my life laid out in front of me and all would be well. I was excited at the prospect of doing something I loved. I applied and was accepted into college to start earning my degree to become a pharmacist. My future was bright—or so I thought!

Within a few months, I no longer had a future. I was eighteen years old and had a cold dose of reality slap me right across the face. I had no clue what to do or where I would turn to next. One can't be a pharmacist when one can't pass basic chemistry. My career as a pharmacist was over before it even started.

We've all had that feeling, haven't we, as though the rug has been pulled out from underneath us and we have nowhere to land.

Here I was, already into my first year of college, and now what? I knew I loved the pharmacy industry. I figured out the next best thing would be to become a pharmaceutical sales rep as I could still be part of the pharmaceutical industry that I loved. I rapidly switched courses, buckled down, and received two degrees: one in marketing and the other in health science.

Then things got interesting. In the months leading up to my graduation, my Cornell University, New York University, Ivy League, super-brainy dad with a PhD in Aeronautical Engineering at twenty (a traditionalist in every fashion and a true rocket scientist) asked me about my job prospects upon graduation.

Job? What job?? According to my father, you needed to have a job offer set up before you graduated college. I had been working hard to find one. I went through all the on-campus job interviews and couldn't find anything. The classic line being delivered to me over and over was I had all the degrees, but I didn't have the sales experience. How do you get experience when no one is willing to hire you?

I vividly remember telling my father, "Dad, I'm trying. I don't know what to do." My dad traveled quite a bit at that time, and he shared an anecdote. "Son, I was on an airplane sitting next to a guy who worked in the office/technology industry. He was in upper management for a copier manufacturer, and we got to talking. He told me to tell you that if you can go out and sell office equipment for a year, you'll get the best hard-nosed sales experience and sales training ever. If you can make it a year, you can parlay that into something else."

I'm taking you back now to January 1988. There was no Internet. So, I picked up the phone book, and I found the biggest ad in the Yellow Pages, called that company and set up an interview. Miraculously, in one week I went through all the interviews with that company. Back then it was easier. As long as you could walk and talk, you could get a job.

The first week after being hired, I sat in a room for five straight days, eight hours a day, watching VHS tapes. I guess that dates me. VHS sales training 101. Nothing to do with office equipment, just sales. By the end of the week, my business cards were ready. They congratulated me and my sales manager gave me my first assignment.

"Starting on Monday, you're going to go out in the field and start making cold calls. But before you do it, we're going to practice what you're going to say. You can't come back into the office until you have gathered fifty business cards. They must have the person's name who's responsible for making decisions, what type of copier they had, and so forth." Old school to the bone, right? Something is telling me this is still happening today!

"Once you come back, you're going to review those names with me. Then you're going to start making phone calls to those people trying to set up appointments."

Seriously, that's how I was trained in this business. Then my sales manager mentioned to me, "Once you set up an appointment, I will go out with you. I will show you how to run an effective meeting, as well as anything else you need to know." Hilarious, I know, as some of this still exists thirty years later!

That first year was the worst time of my life, pure torture, but I kept remembering what my father had told me. If I could last a year in this business, I could parlay it into something else. I kept saying to myself, "I've got to stick through it. I've got to stick through it. I just have to stick through it. I need to grind it out." In that entire year, I made a miniscule $18,000.

My Failure Triggered My Biggest Breakthrough

After that first year, I knew there had to be something better. I had learned the basics, but my education was far from complete. I had learned a long time ago there's no shame in asking for help, but I wasn't getting the help I needed from my first sales manager.

So I decided to become my own sales manager and teach myself. Think about this one for a moment . . . How many of you act as your own sales manager? As an avid reader, I bought every sales book I could afford. I studied them all with the goal of uncovering and implementing two things I learned from every book. What made this special is that through my *Selling from the Heart* podcast www.sellingfromtheheart. net, I would have the opportunity to interview Tom Hopkins thirty years later. His book, *How To Master The Art Of Selling*, was one of the first sales books I read.

I decided to start tracking and monitoring who I was losing to, who the sales reps were, and where they worked. There were a couple of reps I was losing to all the time. I set up a meeting with each one of them to introduce myself and to find out what they were doing differently.

They started sharing with me why they enjoyed working for their respective companies as well as a bit about themselves. Being a high "Type A" person, to begin with, this was music to my ears. The insight into their processes was the start of learning to build professional relationships and one of the best lessons I received.

I took to heart what my father had stressed to me and stuck it out at the first company for a year. The more I learned about the other companies and the family atmosphere they provided, the more I wanted to work there. One of the sales reps I had originally competed against recommended me, and the next thing I knew, I was in sales heaven.

My new company had me shadow one of their top sales reps for ninety days. Not only did I observe what he did, I was also able to ask him tons of questions. After ninety days, I started to get it. I saw firsthand how you could survive in the sales world. I observed how he took care of his clients. I saw his work ethic. I saw how he demonstrated excellence in his performance. He had a system in place, a process, and a plan. I knew if I could model this behavior, I would hit a home run. I've never stopped since. By the way, baseball is my favorite sport!

One of the things I was never coached nor mentored in was the art of building relationships. I was in an industry where equipment broke all the time. It was a high-maintenance, intense type of business, and if you didn't have a well-run service department, sales reps would have to figure out how to deal with customer issues and technical service issues to pacify the customer.

Through all of this, I was learning how to read people. I began to understand them and treated them the way I wanted to be treated. I started to sell to my customers the way I wanted to be sold to.

I went from a newbie making $18,000 my first year to a successful twenty-eight-year career inside the office-technology world. I owe a lot to my dad and the conversation we had back in 1988. It is funny how life works out, isn't it? I am glad those events happened because they've shaped my life in so many positive ways, ways I couldn't even imagine. I can genuinely say I've lived a great sales life.

Stop the Excuse

I believe committing to excellence was the key to unlocking my success back then and I now know that committing to excellence is the key to unlocking success today.

However, I am concerned with the current state of the sales profession. What I'm seeing develop is a lack of commitment to excellence. A culture of excuses and finger-pointing has replaced hard work, grit, and determination. Sales are not easy. Sales are not for everyone, nor for the weak at heart. It requires discipline, determination, and a game plan. It takes a lot out of you, and you must be willing to pay the price, but the rewards are worth it.

If you want to get ahead in life, you must take personal responsibility. You must hold yourself accountable to YOU! It's no one else's responsibility to help you get to where you need to be; it's yours and yours alone. This means that if you had a sub-par month and failed to meet your plan, it's not your manager's fault, your customers' fault, or your prospects' fault—it's your fault! You have to suck it up, self-reflect, buckle down, and get to work. Look at yourself in the mirror and commit to getting better.

No more excuses. No more, "It's Monday. Nobody buys on Monday." "It's Friday afternoon. No one is mentally at the office as they have the weekend on their mind." "It's two weeks before Christmas. Holiday mode has set in." "The competition has better pricing." It's time to suck it up, buck it up, and do your job!

Too many in sales play the deferral game. They play the deflection game as they place the blame elsewhere. A true sales professional takes ownership of everything they do as they facilitate the buyer's journey. If a customer has an issue, it is the sales professional's responsibility to make it right. Sales professionals don't place blame, deflect, or pass problems on to someone else. They serve their clients with the utmost of respect, and they commit to creating an outstanding experience.

Quite frankly, this is the difference between a sales rep and a sales professional. A sales professional finds a way to resolve all of their clients' concerns. They take responsibility for themselves. They figure things out. They do the things others aren't willing to do.

Decision Time

Who are you? Are you an average sales rep doing what you need to do to skate by, moaning, groaning and complaining about aspects of your job? Or are you striving to be a sales professional who achieves their goals and dreams, doing what needs to be done? This means it's your responsibility. It's your responsibility to make the calls. It's your responsibility to prospect. It's your responsibility to learn. It's your responsibility to go above and beyond. It's not anyone else's. You can't wait to be told what to do. You owe it to you, your family and your career!

Here's one thing I need to warn you about this book: I'm not going to hold back. I'm not going to pussyfoot around. I will say the things other people are unwilling to say. I will speak the truth and share what's on my mind.

Let the truth set you free.

If You Want to Be Paid Like a Top Sports Athlete . . .

There's a vast majority of sales reps who seek to get paid sports athletes' wages. The irony is most fail and lack the desire around doing the work necessary to get there. Top professional athletes have no mental excuses or barriers.

Let's look at the life of an average baseball player who starts their career banging around from city to city, living out of motels and surviving long bus rides in hopes they make it to the big leagues to make big money. They're up before anyone else practicing and staying later than anyone else to do the same. They give it everything, they don't give up, and they learn from the process.

When was the last time that you got to work early?

When was the last time you got to work early to do those extras that always need to be done, so the moment the official day starts you're ready to make those phone calls, visit those clients, and take care of any issues promptly? When was the last time you stayed late, working well past 5 p.m., or took a phone call on Saturday because it was in the best interest of your client? These are the things sales professionals don't bat an eye at—they just do them.

It's time to stop making tired excuses like "My clients don't get into the office until 9 a.m., so I won't start my day until then." Or "I am only going to work Friday until 3 p.m. because I know most people have the weekend on their mind." There are no excuses when it comes to your work ethic. I am surprised how many sales reps fail to work a full forty-hour week or can't account for their time. Sorry to burst your bubble! Saying you're out in the field doing stuff doesn't count! Then most of them complain they don't have the money they desire or enough time to accomplish what needs to be done.

What if you're a tenured sales rep with an established client base? What are your excuses? Have you stopped prospecting because you've already "been there, done that" and feel you have earned your sales stripes? Are you relaxing and resting on your laurels? Contrary to what some may think, there's no rank and file in sales.

I love asking tenured sales reps, "What would happen if management came in and said you couldn't sell anything to your current clients for the next six months? For the next six months, all your focus must be on generating new business." What would be their response? Would they rise to the challenge and become better, or would they whine and mope around, looking for the exit door, stage right? Don't get me wrong—your clients are your lifeblood for sales success, but you get the picture!

I can't say this enough: if you want to make serious money, you must get rid of the excuses once and for all. Become serious about your work and put in the time it takes to become a true sales professional.

It's Time for the Real You

I've seen so many salespeople hindered from achieving success because they're trying to be someone they aren't. Have you ever tracked the path of individuals who became successful and tried to mirror what they did, only to achieve lackluster results? Of course, you have.

Want to know why it didn't work? Because your actions were not in line with your core self. You can be true to yourself and be successful. I'm a living and breathing example of it. I have taken all that I have learned over the years, packaged it up, and made it my own. Stay true to who you are. Be genuine, be authentic—get to know yourself. Be curious and ask a ton of questions. Always ask for help. Just be the real deal—the real you!

Whenever someone would ask me, "What are you doing?" my response was always, "I'm just getting it done." Here is what I would like for you to get out of this book: stay true to who you are. Be the real deal, be genuine. Be authentic and sincere, give a rip about your career, and do what you need to do to get things done. Make things happen! Don't become somebody you're not. Don't build a sales lie. Living a sales lie will bite you in the butt every time.

Join me as I take you on a journey to sales success. Throughout this book, we will be looking at what it means to be authentically you and how to use this to brand yourself. We will also be looking at the skills an authentic sales professional possesses, including prospecting and leadership.

I highly suggest that you download The *Selling from the Heart* Self-Reflection Journal at www.sellingfromtheheart.net/

journal that will help you take each chapter and apply it personally.

Are you ready? Are you sure about it? Great! Let's turn the page and get going!

Case Study: C. McCann

Have you ever felt that something was missing, was just off, or you were only going through the motions?

A couple of years ago, I heard Larry speak at an event. He was discussing *Selling from the Heart,* and I remember having my first "ah-ha" moment. I remember asking him about social media and content posts. I told him that I didn't want to share my information about my clients because of my competitors "watching" my every move. He then turned it back around and said, "You don't think they already know that's your client?"

At the end of the day, I know I do a great job for my clients and I was only holding myself back from not promoting their success and the great partnerships I had developed over the years. I decided in 2019 to begin a new chapter. Little did I know at that time in my life that it was a chapter on "me." Somewhere in all the years, I had lost sight of who I was and the real purpose on why I chose a career in sales.

When I started coaching with Larry, he opened my eyes. For so long, I felt I was on a one-way road. I had tunnel vision and stayed in my lane. Over time, I learned that I liked the unknown and winding road. I desired more in my career, and I wanted to be better. I wanted to be great.

I remember one of the first lessons was to go back and actually ask my clients what they thought of me. This was one of those "ah ha" moments. I mean, why didn't I think of that before? I wanted to attract new clients, so why not market my strengths? This is why my clients chose me. That was a turning point for me. After having many conversations with my clients, the same adjectives and phrases kept coming up. An energy and excitement had consumed me. You know that "spark" or "skip" in your step, where you feel on top of the world? My passion had become my purpose. I felt alive, which is a place I had not experienced in a long time.

As I reflect on these past few years, I look at everything I have learned, how I grew, and how I invested in myself. I wish I could tell you that there is some "quick fix." What I can tell you is that if you choose to invest in yourself, you will open many doors. There will be times of very difficult personal growth. You will dig deep and work through emotions. You will fail, and you will fail miserably at times.

However, for me personally, the great success stories outweighed the negative. I learned from every failure and I fine-tuned my technique. I adjusted and asked questions—a lot of questions. I went out of my comfort zone and got familiar with being uncomfortable. I led with my heart and, at times, this left me truly vulnerable. When I stayed true to my beliefs, used transparency, empathy, and provided a customer experience, I was on my *A* game. When I used other techniques that didn't feel right, it left me at a loss. Listen to your instincts; listen to that voice that tells you to demand more. Listen to your clients. If you have a hard time finding your true authentic self, roll up your sleeves and do the work. I promise you that when you find your true passion and desire in your career, it will not feel like work.

It is never too late to start. If you choose to sell with your heart, you will be rewarded in ways that mentally, physically, and emotionally you couldn't imagine. When you choose to be better for yourself and those that surround you, you will feel the change. This change will lead you, ultimately, to your next chapter.

Chapter 1 Summary

- Your story matters but should never hold you back from achieving your sales goals.
- Failure is never final. It is what you learn from it and the actions you take, not to make the same mistakes again, that will create success.
- The only way to be excellent in sales is to stop the excuses and decide to take responsibility for your results.
- You *can* be your true, authentic self and be great at sales.

Don't forget to download your free The *Selling from the Heart* Self-Reflection Journal, at www.sellingfromtheheart.net/ journal, to get the action steps for this chapter.

Brutal Honesty–
It's The Only Way

"Knowing yourself is the beginning of all wisdom."
Aristotle

T im sat at his desk, with his head bowed between his knees, not in prayer but defeat. He had just come back from his monthly sales-team meeting where his name was at the bottom of the sales totem pole for the third consecutive month. He wondered why on earth his company was keeping him onboard, since it was apparent he wasn't producing results.

Alertly, Tim popped his head up as he heard others walking into the sales bullpen. John was high-fived again by everyone for his stellar performance for the sixth month in a row. "How in the heck does he do it?" Tim muttered to himself. "It has to be all luck."

As time went on, Tim's results failed to improve, and desperation set in. He knew his job was soon to be in jeopardy. This sales position meant a great deal to him. He mustered up the courage, swallowed his pride, and struck up a casual conversation with John.

What happened next changed his life forever. John was thrilled to speak with Tim. They arranged to go out for dinner later that night, where they could move the conversation away from prying ears and possible office gossip.

Over a cocktail, John let Tim do most of the talking. Tim shared all the ways he had tried to sell and failed. Toward the end of dinner, John sat back, directly looking right at Tim and said, "I think I have an idea, an inkling of what the problem might be. I want you to think about and digest what I'm about to share with you. Do you really, truly know who you are? From what I am hearing, it sounds like you spend a great deal of time trying to become someone else in sales. Isn't it time you found out how to sell like Tim, the real Tim?"

Tim sat back in total shock. This was the last thing he had expected to hear. He sincerely believed John would share some secret trick, the secret sauce that would catapult him to success.

John sensed Tim still had some doubt, and for the next thirty minutes, he shared what had brought about his success. As the evening wound down, Tim looked right at John and said, "I am going to make a commitment to myself and give what you so kindly shared with me a try. I will follow it to a T," and he did. Within six months, Tim ranked second on his team, right behind John, only a fraction away from surpassing him. You couldn't wipe the smile off his face as he began living his dream.

Chaos and Sales

One of the reasons for Tim's failure is that Tim viewed himself as a sales rep, and John viewed himself as a sales professional. Tim's life was in chaos, and John's wasn't. How do you know if you are a sales rep or a sales professional? The obvious one, plain and simple is results. Lack of results equates to one thing, the need to look in the mirror and create the change!

You're reading this book because you want to become better at the art of sales. The first step is recognizing who you are in the sales world. What do you stand for? One of the main reasons why you may view yourself as a sales rep instead of a sales professional is chaos. Turmoil may have set in within your sales life. Is pure chaos keeping you from seeing the truth and taking the required actions of a successful sales professional?

What does chaos look like inside the mind of a sales rep? Let's look at these symptoms.

1. Only Looking Through Your Own Eyes

Gary Vaynerchuk said something profound in a video I watched, something that really resonated with me.

The issue with salespeople out there, is salespeople are looking at things through their eyes, and their vested interest as opposed to looking at things through their client's or prospect's eyes and their vested interest.

**Sales professionals lead with their hearts!
Sales reps lead with their wallets!**

To me, this is the missing link. Are you looking at things through your own eyes and what's in it for you, as opposed to what's in the best interest of your client or prospect? If so, everything becomes chaotic, since there's no mutual alignment.

2. No Planning

The sales rep wakes up in the morning having no clear understanding of how they are going to start their day. There's no roadmap; instead, they employ a shotgun approach as they just 'wing it.' They should be taking a step back as they ask themselves, "What do I need to do every day and self-reflect upon it?" At the end of a week, "What did I accomplish that got me one step closer to my goals? What must I do the following week?" Put a plan together and work the plan.

This was an integral part of the success I achieved. I never over-complicated anything. There's a quote I love, and I have used it to guide me:

> *If you can't do the little things right,*
> *how do you expect to do the big things right?*

Here is the *big thing*. I believe sales reps' lives are chaotic because very few understand what it really means to be a sales professional. Sales professionals do one thing exceptionally well, one thing that most sales reps fail to adhere to: *hard work!*

3. Lack of Time Management and Patience

These are two things killing most sales reps. All too often they will say they have no time to take appropriate action because of 'stuff,' or should I say the plethora of excuses getting in the way. They fail to manage their time effectively because they don't have a plan or the patience to see the process through, to begin with. They avoid doing what's necessary and then start chasing the shiny bullet to their so-called success.

They have unrealistic expectations. When they start out with their sales career, they observe the actions and results of tenured sales professionals and are quick to get frustrated because they're not producing those same results. It's quite simple: they haven't put forth the necessary time, energy, learning, and practice that sales professionals have.

> **Excuses are a way of saying, "This isn't important to me."**

Allow me to ask you some questions. Are you willing to grind it out and do the hard work? Are you willing to get coaching and training to improve your skills and mindset? You crave big fat commission checks, but are you willing to do the work rather than skate by, doing the least amount of work possible? What's in your wallet? The bank account doesn't lie.

4. Not Doing the Small Things Right

Sales reps' lives tend to be chaotic because some struggle doing the simplest of things correctly. They attempt to cut corners, cheating the system. Their mentality is, how can they get ahead with the least amount of work? When things don't go their way, they complain, moan, and point fingers at everyone else. It's all about taking a real hard look in the mirror! The mirror never lies!

5. You Get Beat on Price

You get beat up on price because you allow it to happen. You let it happen because you fail to understand your why. You don't understand the real and authentic value you bring. Quite frankly, you've trained the buyer to beat you up on price, and you've accepted it.

6. There's No Coaching from Leadership

Sales reps' lives tend to be chaotic because they lack simple coaching from their sales managers. So, just as much as salespeople need coaches, mentors, leaders, and managers within an organization, those same leaders and managers need coaching as well.

Dysfunction is at an all-time high, running rampant, within most sales teams. I call it Isolation Island: upper-level management sitting on one island, mid-level management sitting on another, and the sales team sitting on yet another. You can say they are all consistently inconsistent about any strategic conversation to benefit the entire team.

At best, most sales managers are just delivering messages from upper management. But upper management needs to be coaching, training, and nurturing middle management. Middle management, in turn, needs to be coaching and nurturing their sales reps.

7. Actions Do Not Match Words

Sales reps fail to walk the talk consistently. The BS meters of prospects and clients are at an all-time high. Unfortunately, some people in sales will say whatever they need to make a deal. Buyers have been let down so many times that they have become immune to it and succumbed to the fact most sales reps suck and bring absolutely zero value. When you walk into their office walking, talking, and reeking of commission breath, acting like every other sales rep, they will quickly turn the channel on you just like a bad television program.

8. A Need to Control Everything

Most sales reps are control freaks with massive egos. They've developed a lack-of-trust mindset with everyone around them. In essence, they waste time and energy taking care of things they shouldn't, instead of taking responsibility for the actions necessary to bring in more business.

This was one huge mistake I made—trying to control everything. If there was a billing issue, I needed to make sure I was the one fixing it. If there was a customer service issue, I needed to make sure I took care of it.

Stop it! Become the quarterback and facilitate it getting done by the people inside your company who are responsible for making it happen.

I didn't realize the importance of this until I went to work for a large corporation that forced me to change. "No, you aren't handling that billing issue. No, you're not handling that issue; that's what we have these departments for." What this did was free up my time to develop my business, allowed me to meet with a current client and thereby doing something that was more productive, such as generating business!

I asked a close friend who's in sales how many hours per week he spent on invoicing, billing, or customer-service issues— things that are important but take you away from what you need to do. His answer was astonishing: more than ten hours a week. Stop and think about this one for a moment. Take a forty-hour work week. If you're spending ten of those hours doing tasks others are supposed to because you're a control freak or lack trust, you're losing one whole day a week. You're losing almost a week a month of prime selling time.

Repeat after me: "I'm missing my quota. Why am I missing quota?"

Learn to trust those within your company to do their jobs and use your newfound freedom to become the sales professional's you are meant to be.

How To Get Rid Of Sales Chaos

Is it possible to get rid of personal sales chaos? Yes, it is. Will it be easy? That I can't promise you. Will it be worth it? Yes, yes and YES! You'll be amazed at how different your life will become when you know where you're going and how you're going to get there.

It is a three-step process. You're going to have to get brutally honest about who you are. It comes down to how well you know yourself as an individual. I had Jim Keenan, the author of the book Not Taught, on my *Selling from The Heart* podcast www.sellingfromtheheart.net, and I asked him this question: "What do you think it takes to become successful in sales today?"

He said, "The number-one thing is, you have to become self-aware. You have to get to know you."

To me, that's the single biggest thing, the missing link. If you don't know yourself, how can you go out and prospect for new business?

How can you help your clients? Better yet, how can you do better business? How can you succeed in sales? If you're not self-aware of who you are, how can you become the sales professional you so deserve to be?

The first step is self-reflection.

Without reflection, we go blindly on our way, creating more unintended consequences, and failing to achieve anything useful.
Margaret J. Wheatley

As a sales professional, you must continuously reflect on your performance. What helped you to succeed during the day, week, or month? What caused you to lose a deal? What caused you to win a deal?

Looking at these things helps you to pinpoint your strengths and your weaknesses. What makes you unique? How can you change when you don't know what needs to be done?

Allen R. McConnell, Ph.D., the James and Beth Lewis Professor of Psychology at Miami University, noted the importance of self-reflection several years ago. He said it is also a necessary part of attaining goals, self-improvement, and positive change. For change to occur there must first be awareness—a state of being that can come through self-reflection.

I believe there are two times a day when self-reflection works best: first thing in the morning and toward the end of the day. It depends on whether you're an early riser or a night owl. For me early, and I mean very early, morning works best—3:30 a.m., rise and shine!

I take time each day to think back on the day before, and I ask myself some questions.

- Who am I?
- What am I most proud of?
- What am I most grateful for?
- What did I actually do yesterday?

- What did I learn yesterday that I can apply to today to become a better person?

Self-reflection allows us to understand what's important while focusing on what could be done differently. If you do this religiously every single day, you will start seeing patterns emerge illustrating the things you do well and any possible areas for growth. You will begin to uncover your uniqueness and learn to appreciate it.

Everyone reflects differently, and the way I do it may not work for you. It is OK. Find a method and stick to it. You only need to follow this ground rule: focus on what you do well more than what you fail to do well. When you focus on your strengths, they get better; when you focus on weakness, the mind-screw syndrome sets in, and it gets worse. The only reason you want to look at your failures is, so you don't consistently repeat them.

To get, what you are willing to give?

You should also reflect on your goals. Where do you want to be in one, three, and five years? Include your dreams for your business, your personal life, and your health. This is about you being congruent in all areas of your life. Then start to break down those goals for this year. What can you do this week and this month to make your dream a reality? Self-reflection is a great tool, but only if there are actions put behind it.

Lastly, how are you helping others? Give, and you shall receive. As a sales professional, how are you helping your clients do better business? How are you giving back to the community you live in?

My motto has always been to help first, as this will come back tenfold.

Self-reflect. Ask yourself, "Am I doing what I can in my community to help those in need?" Try giving something back to your friends, colleagues, family, and, most importantly, your clients. Help where they need it the most. Don't ask questions—just do it!

Self-reflection is never easy, but for sales professionals, this is the difference between just getting by and making it happen. Self-reflection is hard work. It's about looking in the mirror, asking the questions, and then answering them. You're in charge of your own sales career.

That leads to the second step in the process, which is self-awareness.

If you're your authentic self, there is no competition. It's quite simple; self-awareness means you know yourself so well that you become amazingly happy. In turn, allowing you to live a wonderfully balanced life.

- Are you living as the real you and not someone else?
- Do your thoughts match your actions?
- Does your walk match your talk?
- Are you emphasizing the positive aspects of your personality?

Living a lie comes out sooner or later. Living a sales lie is even worse, as it will ultimately screw with your career.

Once you know the real you, the fun starts, as you can now begin to craft your sales story. Stories are powerful. They give you a narrative to live by and lessons to pass on shaping the person you are and will become. Your story calls out for your best self. It calls upon you to bring your full attention, strength, and personality to the forefront, creating a life of significance and a career full of abundance.

This requires you to acknowledge the good and the bad within your story. A big part of this is learning how to let go of past guilt, failure, and regret as you start living your life with conviction.

Make a conscious decision today to stop defining yourself by what you're not. Stop beating yourself up (Lord knows, I have learned this the hard way). Every day starts a day filled with new opportunities, so start living a better story.

Self-Awareness Leads to Success as a Sales Professional

Spend any amount of time in sales, and you will have eaten a slice of humble pie and been bitten by the reality bug. This bite injects salespeople with a dose of humility and awareness of their shortcomings, allowing them to become better sales professionals. If you're willing to set aside your ego and to become humble as you go about your work as a sales professional, then you can project an attitude of "others-interest" and thus create a true buyer-focused experience.

Great sales professionals are not self-centered. The best of the best incorporate self-reflection and are truly aware of who they are. They love eating humble pie for breakfast and look forward to a day full of learning as they serve their clients.

A self-aware sales professional reminds themselves on a daily basis, "I don't know everything about my client. So, what will I do about it?

I will stop pretending I know a great deal about my client's business issues. I will strive to be authentic in learning about their problems. I won't pretend that I know!"

I encourage you to stand in front of a mirror and recite these two statements to yourself…

I am a student of my client's problems.

I am an opportunity creator for my clients.

Getting to know yourself allows you to tap into the roadmap known as happiness. This is critical to your success as a sales professional. Your beliefs, your attitude, and your daily routines are mission-critical.

The third step in the process is to challenge yourself.

If you don't challenge yourself, you will never realize what you can become.
TheDailyQuotes.com

Sometimes it's difficult to ask yourself self-directed questions—tough questions that challenge you to become a better person. It's not easy to have these conversations with yourself.

If I can't lead myself, how can I lead other people?

Why is this? Mental barriers such as ego and fear of what may be uncovered prevent some of us from being the best versions of ourselves. The time is now to change all of that!

Are you investing enough in yourself? As sales professionals, we invest so much in making sure our clients are well taken care of that sometimes we forget about ourselves.

Investing in yourself is clearly one of the best returns on investment you can make. Whether it's investing in learning a new skill, developing yourself professionally or personally, or contributing to community service, you need to give to yourself first before you can give to others. Investing in yourself sends a powerful message to yourself and those around you.

A Great Exercise to Challenge Yourself

Set yourself in front of a mirror on a Friday at 5:00 p.m. and answer these questions, "What have I been doing over the last week? What have I been doing over the last month? What have I been doing over the last quarter? Have I been productive? How could I have done my job better?"

It goes back to understanding yourself. How much do I know about my clients? Am I authentic or am I being fake? Over the last week, month, or quarter, have I been a student of my clients' problems? Have I been an opportunity creator for my clients? Or have I just been a whiner and moaner, out there flying by the seat of my pants?

If you can be brutally honest with yourself, if you'll take a step back and ask, "Can I be doing things better than I'm doing now?" Fire yourself on a Friday at 5:00 p.m., self-reflect over the weekend as you create the plan to get your life back in order, and rehire yourself on Monday at 8:00 a.m. and see what happens.

I encourage you to build confidence in your abilities. I challenge you both personally and professionally around these five areas:

- Seek to become an expert in your field of work.
- Constantly crave feedback on YOU.
- Be brutally honest with yourself.
- Set goals and create a business plan.
- Never, ever stop learning.

I encourage everyone to take this seriously. This is what transformed me from a sales rep into a sales professional. It caused me to become more than I could imagine. The opportunity is yours. The question I have to ask is, will you take it, or will you continue to find excuses? The choice is yours.

Chapter 2 Summary

- Chaos in your life leads to poor sales results.
- The signs of chaos are:
  - Only Looking Through Your Own Eyes
  - No Planning
  - Lack of Time Management and Patience
  - Not Doing the Small Things Right
  - You Get Beat on Price
  - There's No Coaching from Leadership
  - Actions Do Not Match Words
  - A Need to Control Everything
- Three steps to getting rid of sales chaos:
  - Self-Reflection
  - Self-Awareness
  - Challenge Yourself
- Challenge yourself in these five areas:
  - Seek to become an expert in your field of work.
  - Constantly crave feedback on YOU.
  - Be brutally honest with yourself.
  - Set goals and create a business plan.
  - Never, ever stop learning.

Chapter 3

Validating Your New Identity

*"If you don't give the market the story to talk about,
they'll define your brand's story for you."*

David Brier

S omething special happens on your journey of self-discovery. You start to become more aware of who you are, and how your uniqueness contributes positively to your clients, your prospects, your centers of influence, and those who know you the best. This is what this chapter is all about— how to share your story in such a way that it positions you as the go-to sales professional that everyone wants to work with.

I must admit something to you. I didn't even know what the word "branding" meant until midway through 2000. It was around 2006, and I hired a business coach. I took it upon myself, investing $10,000 of my own money in coaching, mentoring, and facilitating my journey into discovering what a personal brand was all about. First, everyone has a brand. It's the opinions people form about you that will equate to part of your brand. One simple keyword: it's your promise!

Branding and Your Sales Results

I don't care if you are in sales or not. Just look at your friendships. People are constantly forming opinions of you; look at your inner circle. You may not be selling anything, but those opinions being created about you—that's a brand. Everyone has a brand; either they don't know it, or they don't know what to do with it.

If I were to ask your friends what they thought of you, how they perceive you, what would they say? As a sales rep, you must understand, you do have a brand. You have a story, and it needs telling. This is why it is mission-critical you get to know you. That's why Chapter 2 is so important. If you don't know all of this and you don't know how to market yourself, then guess what happens? People may start creating that brand for you and you will not like it.

> **How do you expect to get noticed in your marketplace when nobody knows you exist?**

Many years ago, I started asking upper-level, mid-level, and lower-level management what they thought of copier reps, as this was the sales channel I grew up in. As one can only imagine, ninety-five percent of the responses were negative, and five percent were positive. Unfortunately, this reflects upon people's perception of the sales profession. If you haven't built and started marketing the brand YOU, then you are labeled, clumped, and lumped within the ninety-five percent. Like it or not perception is indeed a reality in the minds of those that count.

It all goes back to sales reps having a brand; they don't know what to do with, nor do they know how to develop it. Every single day your brand is being built by your actions: how do you interact with your clients? How do you communicate with your prospects? How do you interact with your fellow employees? How do you associate with your manager? These actions are all formulating the foundation of your brand.

This may be one of the hardest things for sales reps to understand, especially in today's business climate, as certain aspects around the modern way of selling hinge upon how well you brand yourself. The biggest problem is most people in sales haven't been taught nor have given thought to how important their brand is and what to do with it.

It is imperative in today's business world for sales reps to learn how to market themselves proactively.

Market Your Value and Uniqueness

This is a tough one for salespeople. It is hard to market yourself and grow your business if you are not clear of the value and your uniqueness you bring to the marketplace. I urge you to go back to your clients who know, like and trust you and ask them, "Can you share with me three ways I have brought added value to your business?" A real gut check time in testing how well you know your clients and how well they know you.

As a young sales professional, if you do not have a client base formed yet, go back to your friends, family or centers of influence and ask them the same question. You can phrase it differently, "What is the value you think I bring out into the marketplace based on what you know of me?"

Broadcast out into the business community your value. Become the difference maker!

The best place to start: go to your current clients and ask for help. Ask them "What words would you use to describe the work I do for you?"

Listen to what they say, as this is one way to build your brand, especially when it comes right from your clients' mouths.

> # Communicate your promise;
> # this is your brand identity.

If you ask most people what adjectives they would use to describe salespeople, you're likely to get, "abrasive, abrupt, annoying, tacky and slimy." There are very few who will say "I had an ambitious sales rep," or "I had an energetic sales rep," or "I had an empathic sales rep," or, best of all, "I had a sales rep who cared and gave a rip about me."

To further understand how to uncover your brand, go to the people who know you well and ask, "What adjectives would you use that best describe me?" Ask the same of five of your closest friends, people in your inner circle, or even your family members.

Understanding how to brand yourself begins with self-reflection, becoming brutally honest with how well you know you. Building your brand is understanding your combination of interests, beliefs, aspirations, values, talent, and skills. All of these personal characteristics bundled together become part of the brand called YOU.

All those characteristics combine to form two words: your promise. It's the pinky swear you have with your clients and what you've developed with your prospects. As you pledge allegiance to your clients and prospects, think about your promises and your brand. This is you to the core.

Once you understand your brand, you can come up with a value statement or vision statement. This is your unique promise of value to your clients and future clients and what you will bring to their organization.

> **True sales professionals take action and promote themselves.**

It goes back to people just wanting the real deal. They want to understand who they're getting involved with. Either you can build a brand or somebody else will create it for you, and we know what happens when somebody else builds your brand. It is not good.

There are some in sales who don't give a rip what their brand says about them, quite frankly, who will know? What they don't realize is that in today's world of Google, your brand is out there for the whole world to discover within seconds. Potential clients or your clients can check you out quite quickly. They can formulate their own beliefs about you many times over before you've even had a chance to share with them who you are or what you are all about.

Think about how you use social media. How do you present yourself out there for the business community to see? When people check you out, do they see someone who is active and shows a professional image, or do they see someone no one follows and pictures of you partying your life away? Become a sales professional who controls and uses social media to position yourself as the go-to person in your niche market. Be intentional about building your brand. Be strategic! Educate, engage and excite people in wanting to get to know the real YOU.

Your Unique Story—The Next Step in Branding Yourself

People relate to stories. Remember back in elementary school sitting cross-legged as the teacher sat in front of the whole class reading a story? Maybe I am dating myself! Now, I'm sure most are following along on their iPads.

Think about it. You're intently listening to the story, and you're creating the pictures of the story as they play out in your mind. How does this relate to sales? Well, you must tell your story or stories in a way that resonates with your clients, through their eyes. This means you must understand their issues, you must understand their concerns, you must understand their initiatives, and you must understand their problems.

Once sales reps uncover this, they can use these stories to share how to solve potential issues or problems effectively. This means you must get better acquainted with your current clients and you must understand the difficulties you've settled for them. Then, use those stories to help as you prospect for new business.

"Mr. Customer let me share with you a story about a client of mine. Their issue was similar to yours, and by the way, I appreciate what you've shared with me thus far. Let me share with you how I was able to help solve it." And the story unfolds. Are you starting to get it?

One thing these kinds of stories do is keep the defensive walls from going up. You've seen it and experienced it. You say the wrong thing or communicate in an offensive manner, and body language starts to change. They're no longer listening to anything you're saying. Stories keep them interacting and prevent the walls from going up. I encourage you to involve them in turning each page of the book as your story continues to unfold.

How to Create Your Unique Sales Story

Here's one great example I enjoy sharing with sales reps. I don't care what you are selling. It can be software, any B2B office product, or telecommunication products: become experienced at using the products you sell. You must use the products in your office. Why? Doing so allows you to create stories around how you are using these products or solutions and how it has changed what you do.

Quite often sales reps are selling things and have no clue how they work or how this affects them. They are selling the theory behind it, but they haven't experienced how it works. How can you tell a story around something you haven't experienced for yourself? What a huge disconnect.

If you're selling software to help reduce the amount of paper someone has in their office, why not personally experience what it can do? Let me share with you what we've done inside our office. Our office used to have twenty-five file cabinets; now it has one. We were able to repurpose our office space and make it more efficient.

A close friend of mine sells wine and spirits for a living. Every Friday, taste tests are conducted within the sales team (now isn't this a real happy hour?). Each team member learns about the product, the story behind it and experiences it personally. This allows them to tell a compelling story behind the product they're selling.

I challenge every sales rep out there to take their top five clients and look at what you've sold to them over the past year. Start learning how this has helped them do their job better. One simple reason: those stories must become the ones told to future clients.

Most in sales sporadically meet with their customers. They fail in continuing to learn about what they sold to them and ask how it has affected their company. How has the product, the solution or the service I deployed inside their office allowed them to do better business? Listen up, take notes, and get testimonials from them. Use these testimonials in assisting you to tell your story.

The Next Step—Validating Your Story

Even if a sales rep has come up with "a story," they fail to capitalize on having it validated. This is one difference between a sales rep and a sales professional. A sales professional backs up their stories with testimonials.

If you look at testimonial, it has the core foundation of money in it, the letters MON.

How do you validate your story? Interview your clients. Sales reps, in general, will say they have great relationships with their clients. Most companies will say they have significant relationships with their clients. Most won't admit they have crappy relationships. A question now arises: how do you know you have a great relationship with your client unless you dig in deep and find out? As I work with sales teams, I always ask them "What do you think is the number-one reason for sales reps not securing more referrals?" Some reps say they don't ask. Some say they try but to no avail. Most have no clue because they never ask. I feel the biggest reason is they don't know their clients as well as they think they do. Fear sets in, they're afraid of their clients saying NO.

I learned the power of testimonials a long time ago. I incorporated testimonies in a way that validated my story. It was through this validation that showed how well I took care of my clients.

It is comical how sales reps are asked to get testimonials. "Go get something on company letterhead sharing how well we're doing." Better yet, some will write these themselves on behalf of their clients thinking this will help them secure more of them. Does craziness happen as you think of where these all go? Possibly in a file folder? Or better yet, it goes into a frame and up onto a customer-acknowledgment wall.

How many sales opportunities are walking into your office now? It would be a safe bet to say, "Not many." Why not get customer-testimonial letters and post these all on your social media platforms, proactively marketing these testimonials? "Here's what people have to say about doing business with me." "Here's what people have to say about how I have helped them solve these issues . . ."

Always be validating your relationships. I always share with salespeople they must start digging in deep with current clients. Start treating them as if you are about to lose them. Interesting concept, isn't it?

One massive disconnect and unfortunate situation I see occurring is when the honeymoon stage is over. The sale has commenced, the commission check was cashed, and what happens to the sales rep? They disappear. The customer is now left asking themselves, "Why did I even get married to this sales rep, better yet, the company? This isn't what I signed up for."

Allow me to ask you a question. When was the last time you did an exit interview? If you're a sales manager, an owner of a company, an executive, or even a sales rep and have lost a current client, how many of you—and pardon the expression, grow a set of cojones? Do you go out and interview, go face to face with curious intent, listen with no set agenda and ask them why they left?

I can guarantee, if you peeled the onion back, all roads point back to the sales rep. This is a tough pill to swallow for most, and why the sales rep must become the quarterback, the on-the-field general. They have to lose control of staying in power over all the side distractions such as invoicing issues, support issues, or even technical issues. Not to the point where they are unaware of them, but they are quarterbacking the entire account. Take the quarterback off the football field and how are you going to run the offense? Take the pitcher off the baseball mound and how is the ball getting to home plate?

They are your customers until somebody comes along and provides them with a better experience.

What would happen to you if you lost your top account? How would this affect you? How would this affect your ability to hit your numbers for the year? Sales reps must understand the reason customers leave. Sure, it may be price, it may be the service department failed to do something, or maybe a problem didn't get resolved in a timely fashion. It is up to you to be the facilitator, making sure it all gets handled correctly.

It's you that brought the company into your organization, but when they decide to leave, you then choose to point the finger elsewhere instead of looking in the mirror. Be comfortable with who you are, take responsibility when you need to, and learn from your mistakes. When you do this, you will have become a true sales professional.

Wow, we've covered quite a bit of material. Let me break it down into a few simple steps. Let loose, get to know yourself, be intentional about building your brand, and create unique stories that sell. Go out and validate those stories by having the courage to interview your clients. If you do these things, I promise you will start to notice greater results, more profitable results. Also, go and download *The Selling from the Heart* Self-Reflection Journal at www.sellingfromtheheart.net/journal. It will have guided questions that will let you go deeper into this material and apply it to your life. Isn't this what it's all about?

In the next chapter, we will look at another essential aspect of finding the authentic you. That is your mindset and how it can either propel you forward or hold you back.

Chapter 3 Summary

- Your brand is formed by the opinions of those who know you personally and professionally.
- You need to know your value and uniqueness to brand yourself as a sales professional.
- You must create your unique sales story that will resonate with the client or customer.
- Then you validate your story by interviewing your clients and get how they feel about you.

Chapter 4

The Hard Work Mindset

"There's no lotion or potion that will make sales faster and easier for you—unless your potion is hard work."
Jeffrey Gitomer

James is a young man with a tremendous amount of potential. From the time he was a young boy, he had the innate ability to connect with and influence people. Everything he did was a success. James was always the top fundraiser in school. He was the best newspaper-delivery person in his community, continually getting massive tips from his happy customers.

When he got his first job at the local burger joint, he was always recognized for his ability to up-sell almost every customer ("Would you like to supersize your fries with that burger?") When he left to go to college, supersize French fry sales hit the burger skid!

It was no surprise James decided to parlay his talents into sales. He earned top marks in his post-secondary education. All of his professors praised him, telling James that he was going to be a rock star. He had no problem securing a job at the company of his choice.

That is when problems started to arise. Everything had always been so easy for James, now he was outclassed, out-muscled and outsmarted. For the first time in his life, he faced rejection. He had always dealt with people one-to-one growing up. Now he was dealing with corporations where more than one person was involved in the buying process.

As time passed, James became slightly depressed and considered hanging it up. His sales manager took notice and took action. He had seen this before with up-and-coming sales rock stars who found the daily sales grind difficult. He knew James could survive if he were willing to learn one vital thing they hadn't taught him in college.

He needed to know how to conquer his mindset. What do you do when your sales career doesn't go the way you had planned? What do you do when you hit obstacles you don't know how to overcome? How do you overcome the negative things that pull you toward quitting?

James had one amazing sales manager, or, I should say, leader. Over the next year, he mentored James, helping him focus on the areas holding him back. As time unfolded, James soared as top sales professional in his company.

Why Your Mindset Is Important in Sales

All too often, we beat ourselves up. We turn the mental hammer on ourselves when we feel like we're getting beat up by our clients and prospects. Then our sales managers hammer on us about what we're doing wrong as opposed to what we're doing right.

I will share an example from my own experiences. In a previous company I worked for, it was apparent they had grown to accept the fact I was going to make quota month after month, year after year. They knew I had phenomenal relationships with my clients. They assumed I could do everything and never asked if I could use any help. You could say I was on sales autopilot. Does that sound familiar? How many of you are operating in autopilot mode?

Then something changed. A new sales manager was brought in and immediately focused in on my weaknesses, never acknowledging my strengths. Even though my sales performance hadn't dropped, he was always on me. Was I really that bad? Maybe I wasn't that good? I became my own worst critic. I let that Debbie-Doubter mindset start to control my life.

I know we've all been there. Before you know it, you find yourself in a deep, dark hole and you don't know how to crawl out of it. You find yourself there because of the mental beating you've placed on yourself. How do you fix it? Surround yourself with positive people, ones you can trust. Create an inner circle of mentors, friends, and family who want to see you succeed.

Focus on the people who know you well, the ones you can open up to and share what's on your mind. Intently listen as they share ideas of how to help. Become vulnerable and open up your mind, as this doesn't make you a weak person. The most successful people have coaches. Everybody needs that person or group of people they can hold themselves accountable to— who sees you as you truly are, knows your weaknesses, and understands your strengths. The people who say, "Let's figure out what the problem is and let's come up with an action plan to help you move forward."

The Rejection Factor

Let's face it: in sales, we get a ton of rejection. You've got to be strong-minded, strong-willed, and thick-skinned. I don't care what kind of sales it is—it could be low-end B2B or complex B2B—you get beat up, and you must be able to handle it, take it in stride.

Just like a football player who gets the snot beaten out of him, maybe the wide receiver who runs the route and gets sandwiched in the middle of the field. They must shake it off, hop back up, and get back into the game. That's what needs to happen in sales.

It has happened to us all when rejection starts to play with our minds. Instead of working your business plan, you begin to 'shotgun' things as you start seeing fewer results. Things start to fall apart because you've allowed it to happen; you've let the 'rejection bug' get inside of you. The best thing you can do is learn to let it go and never let it in.

Rejection is not directed at you. There are many other circumstances behind it or reasons for a client rejecting what you have to offer. You can never take rejection personally.

Early on in sales, I would take everything personally. I would allow rejection to eat at me, getting the best of me. I would take someone not doing business with me as a reflection of my skills. I even took the blame for things that were going on inside the client's office. I know what you may be thinking: Larry is one weird dude! I was just so eager to please that I accepted everything as being my fault.

There were a couple of things that helped me overcome this dreaded disease. First, I learned how to develop a positive mindset. I learned to feed my mind with positive thoughts which caused my mind and my skills to grow. Secondly, I became a voracious reader. Let me ask you a question. Before you picked up this book when was the last time you read to nurture your mind? If it has been longer than two weeks, please find the time in your schedule to read, learn and grow. Develop a learning mindset. I know you're capable of cultivating it.

Sales Reps Today Have Hypnotized Themselves

If you think about this quote at its core, if you get down to the root of all of the issues sales reps have, it boils down to one thing: are you prospecting? Or are you not prospecting?

If we look at sales today, sales reps are reading and listening to advice that cold-calling is dead. No one picks up the phone; everyone hides behind their e-mail. Sales reps start listening to this nonsense and internalize it. In today's sales climate, sales reps can't go a day without seeing an article on the internet justifying how cold-calling is dead. "In today's business world, *this* is how you should be prospecting." It just plain confuses sales reps to the point where their minds become paralyzed.

> **Sales reps have hypnotized themselves into believing what they aren't doing doesn't work.**

The scarcity mindset limits your ability to accomplish great things. When you believe there are only one or two ways to develop business and you're not good at either, then you stop taking action. It all boils down to lack of practice as you confront this question: am I a sales rep or a sales professional?

It doesn't matter if it's outbound, inbound, all-bound, traditional, modern, social; you must use every single prospecting tool available when it comes to developing your business. This is why I say sales reps have hypnotized themselves into believing what they aren't doing doesn't work! How many sales reps genuinely have a rock-solid plan to build their pipeline? Most don't. Then they start reading articles all over the Internet that have them saying "Hey, Ms. or Mr. Manager. I shouldn't do it, because here's a stack of PDFs reciting cold-calling is dead."

They create a mindset that most methods don't work and then use that as an excuse for not achieving sales success. It is time that changed!

Throughout this book, I will introduce you to some awesome people who have made a difference not only in my life but in the lives of others. The first one is

Other Mindset Issues

The first is a *victim mentality,* and this applies to those who place the blame on others. They deflect. They enjoy playing the role of a martyr. They focus on coming up with excuses, explaining why it isn't their fault.

The higher the tenure, the better the 'reasons' get. I have heard some that are very believable until you realize you've been hearing these same old excuses for years. Then you see the truth.

Next is *not believing in yourself.* Sometimes even I fall prey to this. It's self-doubt, the mental giant, beating up on you with the psychological hammer. You start saying to yourself, "Maybe I'm not cut out for this." Before you know it, you've spiraled down into a deep dark hole, and then what do you do? You either find a way to climb out, or you succumb.

I believe a significant reason salespeople stop using or become afraid of the phone is they had a bad experience early on and said to themselves, "The phone is horrible." I've had friends who've left sales positions because they were petrified to use the phone. Not that they weren't good at sales; they were just scared to use the phone.

I think another mindset holding people back is *constantly complaining*; they see everything in a negative light. I've seen this time and time again. They complain about everything. They complain about the compensation program, they complain they don't have enough leads, they complain they don't have enough clients; they are constantly grumpy.

Why are they complaining?

It goes back to lack of practice, planning, and preparation around the core requirements of their job. They have no written roadmap or a simple plan They're not working at it every day. There's too much 'winging it.' Then when sales reps start losing deals, complaining sets in. "I lost because of the price. I lost because…" Fill in the blank with all of the lame excuses. You lost because you got outsold. You lost because of YOU!

You're complaining because you're not doing your job. You're not working on it every day. You're not working your plan.

Next is the fear of change. Many times, this applies to sales reps who have been at it for years. They are dead set in their ways. Ask them to do one thing outside what they've been doing, and they start crying about it. They ramble on, saying,

"You know what? I've been doing it this way forever, just leave me alone."

Here's a classic example. I was conducting a workshop with a sales team. It was a combination of newer sales reps and very seasoned ones. The younger reps were intently engaged, taking notes like crazy and carefully absorbing what I was sharing. The tenured reps had their arms crossed, mentally telling themselves, "Been there, done that, and why in the world am I here?" I know you all get what I am saying! I saw it with their body language.

Even though we were talking about social aspects and online methods to help enhance their business, their ego filled attitudes said, "I've been doing it this way, and it works. Why would I want to change? Just let me be."

A closed mind is a death sentence for sales reps!

Folks, I don't care how long you have been in sales—everyone can learn something new!

I understand the tenured sales rep mind; most are dead set in their ways, and I get it. However, they're the ones who have the most to lose. What happens if they lose one of their largest accounts? Then what happens? What would they do? They would have to go back out and start prospecting, something they haven't done for quite some time and something management has allowed them to get away with it. Don't hate on me; I'm just speaking the truth.

Fear of change and **ego** are the two biggest things holding sales reps back. "What happens if this modern stuff doesn't work? I don't want to be exposed." So, they just wing it. "I will get by with my charm and B.S. my way through this." I hate to tell you this, but it just doesn't work any longer. People can see right through it, especially the buyers of today.

All this leads to them *giving up*. I firmly believe it's the fear-of-change mindset that causes sales reps to give up or stop trying. "I'm not going to learn anything new—I'm going to throw my hands up. I'm going to try to skate by in hopes I can somehow just squeak by."

All of these things play out with sales managers as well. A primary reason these things exist with sales reps is sales managers haven't brought it out into the open, coaching them differently. The sales monsters being created can be attributed to . . . who else? Yes, their sales managers and their enabling ways.

Ask a sales manager why their sales team is only at fifty percent of the plan. They will start to point the blame at others. They start complaining. They don't believe in themselves. They possibly go on to say, "Oh, well, this thing happened . . ." "It was due to a bad quarter because... " Fill in the blanks with excuses.

These mindsets holding sales reps back can be directly attributed to one thing: the difference between sales managers and sales leaders. Are they helping their reps do their job better? Are they sitting down with their reps and proactively engaging in helpful conversation?

Let's take sports: you have the head coach, but they are also the team leader. If they notice spotty performance, or they notice somebody having a bad game, what happens? They pull the player into their office and start coaching them along. They start discussions with them about the issue with positive affirmation as they hold them responsible for getting better.

Another mindset issue: *knowing it all.* "Don't tell me what to do; I already know everything." "Don't tell me how to prospect; I already know how to prospect." Well, if you knew how to prospect, you would have a bigger sales funnel. "Don't tell me I need more appointments; I know I need more appointments." Then why don't you have them?

This is just as bad as complaining, not believing in yourself, and fear of change. These reps are the ones who usually know the least, and they cover it up with false bravado.

One last one: *trying to impress.* They wear the nice watch. They drive the nice car. They wear the nice suits. They're trying to impress, making everyone think they're successful. It goes back to being insecure with themselves. They're trying to get by on charm and sophisticated conversations with people. Fake news, fake sales reps!

Me, I always kept my mouth shut and did my job. I went about doing everything silently and let my numbers speak for themselves. I was the first one in the office in the morning, working on my plan. Then I left the office, I went out in the field, and I did what I was supposed to do. I was consistent with my numbers every single time because I put in the work. I did my job!

The Solution

If you saw yourself in any of these examples in this chapter, it's time for you to start having a serious talk with yourself. It's time for you to start building you. How do you that?

Start by setting appointments with yourself. Acknowledge you are important and start making daily appointments with YOU! Mark it on your calendar. Mentally phone yourself every day, first thing in the morning. Think about it—there's no gate-keeper except the mental one.

- Set the mental timer daily and when the time comes, don't miss it!
- Set an appointment with yourself to read for fifteen minutes.
- Set an appointment with yourself to exercise.
- Set an appointment with yourself to write thank-you notes to your friends, people who mean a lot to you, and, more importantly, your clients.
- Set an appointment with yourself to uncover what you could be doing better.

If you don't take care of yourself, how can you take care of your clients?

Sales remind me of the National Football League. It's a smash-mouth, in-your-face, full-contact business sport. You will be knocked down, and you must get back up. You must handle rejection and brush it off, just like a quarterback sack.

How many calls do you need to make to set up one quality appointment? I don't care if the number is twenty-five, fifty or seventy-five; it's downright tough! The best call you can make is to yourself. I guarantee you will get through one hundred percent of the time!

Investing in yourself gives the single best return on investment. Invest in learning a new sales skill. Invest in developing yourself personally and professionally.

Invest in hiring a coach or mentor. Invest in building better relationships. Invest in yourself and stay true to you!

You must give to yourself before you can give to others. This takes personal commitment, but the rewards . . . they are well worth it.

The Outcome of Investing in You

Sales today is more competitive than ever. Look no further than to professional sports. How hard is it to repeat as champions? It's extremely challenging, as other teams raise their game to take down the champions. Are you starting to get it? You must stand out from the competition now more than ever, as a sales professional. One of the most effective ways to make this happen is to invest in yourself and your career.

Consider making the investment in enhancing your skill set and what this could mean to your sales career today, tomorrow, and well into the future.

Areas this could impact:

- **Potential earnings**—Enhancing your professional skills can translate to higher pay and commissions.
- **Job growth**—Making an investment and gaining expertise in what you do allows you the opportunity to move into more advanced sales roles.
- **Job knowledge**—Always be learning. This allows you to stay at the forefront of your industry. Learning new techniques can have an immediate impact on your job.
- **Leading and motivating others**—An investment in yourself may even help you transition into a leadership role. Think of the impact you could have on others as you inspire those around you to reach for higher goals. Investing in yourself packs a powerful punch!

It allows you to become the best version of yourself. As you invest in yourself, watch out for the opportunities that come your way and the people who start turning to you.

This is one sales appointment you must not procrastinate in making!

What's next? We'll work on specific skills that are going to help you move your business forward. I encourage you to get the *Selling from the Heart* Self-Reflection Journal at www.sellingfromtheheart.net/journal. It will help you to apply what you have learned in this book and become a better sales rep or manager.

I am where I am in my career because I learned I couldn't do this on my own. I have people I have learned from over the years, who've coached me, mentored me, and set me on the right path. Now, it's time for me to pay it forward. I would like to do the same for you.

Case Study: J. Collins

I met Larry Levine about two years ago. At the time, it was one of the most interesting meetings I ever had. A friend of mine named Chris had posted a copy of a signed book on LinkedIn. The author had actually taken the time to sign the book and comment on Chris's LinkedIn post—it was awesome! I couldn't believe a sales expert would go out of his way to sign a book for Chris and then actually show that he appreciated him by sharing it on LinkedIn; I had never seen anything like it! I liked the post, as it really struck a chord with me. Within a couple of hours of liking that post, the author reached out to connect with me on LinkedIn and inquired if his book would resonate with my sales team. From there, we've built a terrific friendship and a mutually beneficial business relationship. What stuck with me then and now, two years later, is that I understand Larry is a real person, and everything he does starts with *Selling from the Heart*.

Sales isn't something that is taught in many schools. It's not something that many people aspire to do. Why is that? The obvious answer is that it's because we have seen this job done so poorly time and again in our lives. We've encountered a salesperson who we knew didn't care or appreciate us as human beings, but rather just as potential commission for them. This has led the majority of society to despise salespeople, as opposed to appreciating them for their expertise, sound advice, and providing solutions to our problems. Most people don't appreciate salespeople because they reek of "commission breath." The problem with sales in the world today is that it's just an end to the means, meaning people do it just to get paid. In their relentless pursuit of the dollar, they sell out and will be whoever they think the prospect wants them to be, never being authentic and, therefore, never being themselves.

I've worked in sales in sports and entertainment for two decades now. In that time, I have worked with countless sales trainers and experts, people I like and respect very much. That said, if there was one knock, I'd put on a lot of the training that's delivered in this industry is that we are taught to be a very specific way in our approach and delivery. That's not to say entry level sales reps in sports don't need direction; they need a lot of it. But in much of the training we are provided, we lose our own voice and never properly learn how to communicate in an authentic manner. Larry's entire philosophy in Selling from the Heart is that the prospect will always buy from people they like and trust—that's a given; but they will like and trust us because we as sellers are real about who we are and how we communicate with people.

I'm the senior director of Ticket Sales and Staff Development for the Los Angeles Kings and AEG Sports. In my position, I am responsible for training our young sales professionals to grow in their roles and hit our ticket goals while doing so. I brought Larry in a couple of times over the past two years to work with our teams. He first came in and talked with our AHL affiliate, the Ontario Reign, and later to work with our staff at the LA Kings. In the past, both the Kings and the Reign had worked with some incredible sales trainers and consultants on growing the skillsets of the staff. We had some very good and professional sellers on our staff who did an incredible job.

On the opposite end of the spectrum were many younger sales reps who were struggling to find their own voices and to communicate in a manner that they were comfortable with. They were focusing so much on what to say and how to say it that they were not being themselves, and their sales performance (or lack thereof) was evidence of it. They were uncomfortable and confused, and we had to make some changes. I knew that I needed to change the message they were hearing and provide them with an extreme concept suitable for sports: *be yourself!* We've changed a lot of how we train by utilizing Larry's message, and great things are happening because of it.

Selling from the Heart is all about being yourself. It means gaining confidence in who you are because you are a true professional. It means caring about the person as a human being, not just a sales prospect. It means spending the time and energy to improve your prospect's lives. After working with Larry for the last couple of years, it's a point I've made daily to reinforce our staff. I'm excited to be a part of Larry's sales revolution and continue to push the message of authenticity in this industry. As you read this book, you'll gain an understanding of what being authentic can do to revolutionize your sales efforts and who you are as a sales professional. Good Luck!

Chapter 4 Summary

- Your mindset is essential for sales.
- Rejection is a part of sales, and you must learn to get over it.
- When you believe there are only one or two ways to develop business and you're not good at either, then you stop taking action.
- Mindset issues you may face:
  o Victim mentality
  o Not believing in yourself.
  o Constantly complaining
  o Fear of change.
  o Fear of ego
  o Giving up.
  o Knowing it all.
  o Trying to impress.
- Start by setting appointments with yourself.
- Acknowledge you are essential and start making daily appointments with YOU!

Section 2:

The Sales Skills of An Authentic Sales Professional

What Consistent Prospecting Looks Like

"Sales professionals do consistent prospecting; sales reps do inconsistent prospecting."

Larry Levine

The biggest problem with salespeople today is they're consistently inconsistent with how they go about developing their business. The root of all sales evil is an empty pipeline. The reason why an empty pipeline exists is your fault. Not your company's fault or anyone else's. It's the failure to make a non-negotiable deal with yourself, repeating to yourself every single day I must set aside the time to prospect.

I don't care how long you've been in sales. I don't care how many current clients you have. Failure to prospect is going to come back and bite you in the rear end, sooner or later. It will rear its ugly head as it starts playing with your mind.

This is the single biggest issue with salespeople. I don't care how you refer to yourself, a sales rep, a sales professional, or even a major account executive. An empty sales funnel and nothing in their pipeline is the reason why sales reps complain and moan about their commission checks and comp programs.

It all boils down to a few things, lack of practice, laziness, poor management, and a reactive, not proactive, approach to prospecting.

Lack of Practice

> No one in your pipeline = Poor Productivity =
> Empty Wallet = No Bank Account

Ask sales reps, "What's the hardest part of your job?" What do you think the first answer that comes up is?

Prospecting

To prospect, you must be able to engage in and start a conversation with somebody. All too often, I observe sales reps 'skating by' just doing enough to generate the bare minimum required to produce sales. What's worse is some will even go as far as complaining to the point that management enables and fosters this behavior by assigning accounts to them. All this, so they don't have to work as hard, justifying their existence.

Lord forbid, ALL those in sales do the core foundation of what they were hired to do!

Instead of practicing to become better at prospecting and really knocking it out of the ballpark, many rely on 'only' having conversations with their current clients. They become highly over-compensated babysitters. They don't even ask for referrals or attempt to generate new business. It gets to the point where they can't figure out how to have an effective conversation with anyone outside of their client-base, because their entire focus has been on people who know them, not augmenting their skills with people who don't know them, a.k.a. prospects.

I came out of the copier channel. It's a bit old school, highly traditional, laggard in nature channel, but still alive and well. But for me, prospecting from the 'get go' is the number one thing even after all these years. It's the thrill of the hunt, the thrill of the next great conversation, the next great relationship. I've made a non-negotiable deal with myself that every single day I must have a new conversation with somebody. Every single day I have to block out time to prospect.

Throughout my sales career, I didn't have a marketing department, I didn't have a business development representative, I didn't have an account development rep nor a sales development rep. I didn't have a telemarketer. I didn't have any of this; I was solely 100 percent responsible for my own pipeline.

A true sales professional doesn't rely on anyone else to help them prospect nor add to their pipeline. They must prospect themselves. This is a tough pill for most to swallow and to realize. You don't earn your tenure stripes in sales to the point where prospecting becomes 'I'll get around to it later'. Because quite frankly, "What makes you any different than any other sales rep in your office?" Nothing, my friends, get over it!

Laziness

There are sales channels that are very successful integrating the use of SDRs, BDRs, ADRs or whatever the acronym you want to use that will help kick-start sales opportunities. They pass off "qualified leads" to salivating sales reps and overtime these sales reps become trained like Pavlov's dogs. These reps unfortunately become dependent on this activity as their sole source of filling their funnel. They don't prospect for themselves as they become inflicted with the dreaded disease known as "Lackitus Prospectitus."

Use this as gravy. The icing on the cake. Don't get me wrong. I've been in situations where I've had a telemarketer before and have had leads passed on to me. Of course, I'm not going to look a gift horse in the mouth, but I'm sure not going to rely on it as my sole source of filling my sales funnel.

A sales professional takes a proactive approach in filling their sales funnel. It's a non-negotiable pact they make with themselves. They say to themselves, "I am responsible for my sales funnel. I am responsible for the health of my sales funnel. If there's nothing in my sales funnel, then it's my fault." It all boils down to one word, prospecting.

Poor Management

Start peeling back most sales reps' funnels, and most go out one, two or three months, if they have anything in their funnel at all. It's no fault of the sales reps because those in sales management have fostered environments where they allow inconsistent prospecting. Poor funnel management in the here and now is all that is focused upon. It's unfortunate, but this has become the nature of the beast.

Take a rep who has been in sales less than a year, less than six months, most sales managers beat on them and hound on them around prospecting. Prospect, prospect, prospect. Get out in the field! Stir the pot, make it happen, turn over some rocks.

Get new accounts! Grin, grunt and grind it out. Prospecting is the number one thing that you do.

Then as these young reps start prospecting like crazy . . . they return to the office after a long day of prospecting and observe tenured sales reps who've become lazy, complacent, egotistical desk jockeys babysitting a list of current clients.

Then young sales reps start muttering, "Why am I doing all of these things as these tenured sales reps aren't doing any of it?" I am being polite as I am sure there may be some other colorful language in this as well.

This environment has been fostered by management and over time young sales reps start mimicking the behavior of others. They start building an account base, they start managing the account-base, they start flipping the account-base and then before you know it the vicious cycle repeats itself year over year. The worst part, management allows it to happen.

In my opinion, sales management has blown it because they've fostered the behavior of inconsistently monitoring how all sales reps are prospecting. Why just focus on the thirty and the sixty days? Why not more?

Ask any sales rep, tell me what you're going to close nine months from now? You'll get blank stares and you'll hear a needle hit the floor. Why? Because no one is thinking of prospecting nor relationship building past the small window called thirty days, sixty days and ninety days.

Many sales reps fail to prospect looking to start conversations as they reactively prospect looking for somebody to buy something right now. Why not both? They prospect just long enough to find those who want to buy, doing enough to hit quota. Then they stop then start the prospecting engine just long enough as they attempt to hit quota again. Which leads to . . .

Reactive Instead of Proactive Prospecting

The average sales rep reacts to an anemic sales funnel, because they fail to make prospecting a non-negotiable daily activity. Instead, they drum up excuses and then when crunch time comes, they panic; go into desperation mode as they kick it into overdrive putting three months' worth of action into two days and fail.

What Sales Professionals Do

To me a sales professional does the complete opposite than that of the average sales rep. They're proactive, they're offensive minded about prospecting. A sales professional operates as if they're the CEO of their own business, where an average sales rep operates as if they are an employee of the business. It's an interesting way to look at it. But it's all mindset.

A sales professional truly loves what they do and takes their profession to heart. An average sales rep operates as an employee in a business doing the bare minimum expected in order to get by and collect a wage. Sales professionals are proactive in how they grow their business and proactive in how they operate their business. They are always on the offense, and they know how to play defense.

They're always out there operating with a non-negotiable mindset, especially when it comes to prospecting. Sales professionals say to themselves, "What am I doing to open-up new conversations every day?" "What am I doing on a daily basis to consistently groom and nurture my client relationships?"

To me this is the mark of a sales professional. What do I have to learn today? What am I going to read today? What am I going to do to enhance my relationships with my clients? For me, the simplest way a sales professional prospects, is that they prospect through their client-base. They build rock-solid, credible relationships with their current clients, and they proactively ask for referrals. These are the best kind of referrals. These are introductions into their networks, introductions into conversations with others based upon trust and credibility. Isn't this fantastic top-of-the-sales-funnel work?

Networking and connecting becomes a consistent part of a sales professional's life. They build great inner circles and in turn help connect others. They leverage their client networks and they ask their clients for help. A sales professional asks to be introduced to their clients' centers of influence: to the people they know, the people they hang out with.

I am always asking my clients, who do they know? Who could they introduce me to, to help fuel a conversation by becoming that bridge, becoming a conduit?

Conversely, if you're going to be proactive inside your client base, then helping your current clients, becomes of the utmost importance. Ask yourself, how are you going to help them grow their business? How are you going to bring your centers of influence, connect them with other people that you know? Are you bridging current clients through introductions? How can you help them grow their business? Your clients are buying services from other people and other organizations. There might be something you know that can help them.

Start prospecting through your client-base, but also interact with them to help them do better business. I believe it's a two-way street. That's what sales professionals do as they bridge the hearts and minds of others together.

Sales professionals control what happens inside their sales funnel. It's all up to them, nobody else. Let's use sales quotas as an example. I always worked things backwards. If I needed to hit $100,000 a month as the benchmark, then based on my marketplace, based on my current clients, based on developing business, then what do I need to do on a daily, weekly, monthly basis to hit my quota number?

I take into consideration my compensation program. If I just do the bare minimum and I hit $100,000 a month in sales revenue, for instance, then based on my compensation program I am going to make "X" amount of dollars. What happens if I want to increase my earnings by 25 percent? This means I have to break through the glass ceiling of whatever my quota is. If my quota is $100,000 a month, and I want to make 25 percent more, this means that now I have to look at driving $125,000 worth of business.

It's a numbers game, because to reach $125,000, you have to make a certain amount of sales. To make those sales means you have to do so many qualified meetings. To get those meetings you need to do "X" amount of calls, speak to "X" amount of people in order to coordinate these meetings. Then break this down into how many you have to do every day, week after week.

Two Different Ways to Prospect

My biggest concern with the state of sales, when it comes to prospecting is everyone is spouting the old way is dead. It just doesn't work anymore. You don't understand that the newer generation doesn't use the phone, they use everything else but. The issue is at a certain point in time you are going to have to use the phone and this generation has not been taught basic phone skills, let alone how to sell over it.

Larry Levine

The bigger controversy is what's more effective. Offline/face-to-face prospecting or online/social media prospecting. The answer is a combination of both. If you want to be successful in sales today, you must become efficient and effective in tying all of these together. No questions asked, it's non-negotiable. Let's take a look at each one and the role that it plays, plus some examples from two friends of mine of how you can apply this to your prospecting efforts.

Offline/Face-to-Face

Face-to-face prospecting is not dead. It is still alive and well. The only difference is you must adjust it according to the market.

For instance, in a big city, it may be difficult to gain success in face-to-face prospecting. Using social networking and business events such as those held by the local chamber of commerce, (yes, they still do work) can bring success. Attend social gatherings. Salespeople fail to realize they can prospect in social gatherings by simply starting conversations. This can even be done quite effectively at community events.

"The art of conversation lies in listening"
Malcolm Forbes

Salespeople must always have the "prospecting light" shining bright inside their head. When one considers face-to-face prospecting and the methodology behind it, what comes to mind? Traditional cold calls, and every sales rep knows what traditional cold calling is all about. Pulling doors, door knocking, glad handing, whatever you want to call it. That's just good old-fashioned prospecting.

This is what makes most people in sales cringe and have their stomachs turn in knots. But cold calling still works. It's not dead. Far from it. It just depends upon your marketplace.

If you are in small-town USA, or small rural areas, you can still pull off prospecting face-to-face quite successfully. Conversely, in large metropolitan cities it's more difficult to prospect face-to-face. Your return on effort is not very high, but you're still going to have to do it.

The one thing you can't call face-to-face prospecting is randomly passing out business cards. This is a useless activity as no relationships are being developed. Today's sales economy is based on the credible and heartfelt relationships you form, and this takes time.

Face-to-face prospecting works best when you develop a positive mindset. In today's current sales climate, salespeople just don't think face-to-face prospecting works with any level of success. They equate face-to-face prospecting with cold calling, and thus, the plethora of excuses follow. Inconsistent prospecting leads to inconsistent and spotty results. Get back to practicing!

A young sales rep equates face-to-face prospecting to cold calling, pulling doors and passing out business cards.

A sales professional will equate face-to-face prospecting to business development or networking. They become actively involved in community groups. They consistently interact within their centers of influence. They get to know their city officials. They become strategic with how they may use face-to-face prospecting and how they view prospecting in order to develop relationships.

Let's face the facts, it's harder to walk into offices now and talk to the decision makers. People are too busy to be interrupted to have a conversation. This doesn't mean you shouldn't do it. You can still visually observe what's going on inside the office. Things you can't see through your social goggles. You can still gather a name or two, maybe even drop a strategic marketing piece off or case in point: my friend, Dale Dupree!

Dale makes face-to-face prospecting absolutely hilarious and busts the ice with people in doing so. It's that person who meets and greets you that will either make or break you moving forward.

You can act like a sales rep or you can act like a sales professional when it comes to prospecting. You can stand out from the sea of sameness by being unique. Do something different, become memorable when you're prospecting.

How Do You Prospect Online & Through Social Media?

This is an interesting question . . . I enjoy listening to the banter with the sales teams I work with when I ask, "Has prospecting become easier or harder over the last five years?"

Ten plus years ago, there weren't as many ways to prospect as there is now. In my opinion, prospecting today has become easier. There's so much information out there to allow sales reps to do their job better. I believe listening has become the new prospecting.

What I mean by this is whether it be through the use of social media sites, such as LinkedIn, Twitter, Instagram or Facebook, a sales professional will integrate the use of these platforms to listen, observe and learn more about their clients and prospects online. They will strategically engage, educate and create awareness on these platforms as an additional methodology around driving conversations.

This becomes an augmented prospecting approach, based upon the social channels your clients and buyers hang out on.

These social tools leveraged correctly, integrates strategically into a business development cadence.

You're still going to use the phone. You're still going to use email. You're still going to use networking and community events. You're still going to leverage referrals. But social media has opened up a whole plethora of new business opportunities and new ways of connecting.

Allow me to introduce you to my friend Kenny Madden www.linkedin.com/in/kennymadden.

Kenny with such brilliance illustrates the #socialphone, a blending of cold calling with social selling to infuse modernization into traditional prospecting. He refers to this as smashing with absolute discipline the very best of Email, InMail, Voicemail, LinkedIn, Twitter, Facebook, Instagram into one beautiful integrated approach. "The social phone."

Social Window + Social Phone + Social Selling = Enhanced Sales Funnel

The social phone allows you to listen and communicate with the voice of your clients and prospects. By engaging in online conversations and leveraging social networks, you create the opportunity to listen to the voice of your potential clients. The more intimate, authentic, genuine relationship you can establish, the more loudly you'll hear their voice.

What's nice about the modern business world is there are a multitude of ways to open new conversations and new relationships with people. Real-life networking or out in the field prospecting still has its place, but social media has opened up a new world of possibilities for meeting potential new clients.

All day, every day think of social media and how you use it as your online trade show. LinkedIn becomes your online stage, your brand, your samples can be content as this provides you with an air of validity. It's a perfect way for your prospects and clients to check you out and to discover more about you.

> ***Is your social window open for business, closed for business or is it in need of tenant improvements?***

There needs to be a mindset and skill set paradigm shift from how most sales reps are attempting to use social media albeit unsuccessfully at best. When we recognize social media is not our primary prospecting mechanism but simply augments prospecting, it changes our approach as this is integrated into our sales strategies.

Socially Adjust Your Mindset

Getting in front of a potential client for a first meeting now requires socially adjusting your mindset. This means adjusting your prospecting strategies as:

- Prospects require a higher level of introduction before granting a sales call
- Prospecting in person and online is essential to sales growth
- Prospecting development and nurturing relationships must be practiced with patience and reeled in with conversation
- Being relevant and memorable is the new differentiator
- Becoming visible, vocal and valuable is a must

Our business world is constantly changing. Social media is a critical part of selling, particularly in the modern digitally enhanced business world; social selling techniques alone won't get you the success you deserve.

When it's all said and done it's about the smashing of all the different ways to prospect into the social phone. Everything revolves around the art of a conversation. The misconception is that online and social media is the panacea solving all of your sales woes. Well, I have news for you: if you stink at regular prospecting, you're going to stink at prospecting and leveraging social media. There's no way around it.

If you're successful with face-to-face prospecting, if you're successful with driving phone conversations, then social media becomes just another outlet. I'm not saying one is better than the other, as you must use every single prospecting tool available in order to do your job better.

I grew up in a sales world where outbound prospecting, face-to-face prospecting was all I could do. I grew up in a time that all I had was a phone, period. There was no computer. There was no email. There was nothing. It was my ability to pick up the phone, generate interest and in turn secure a face to face meeting.

What If You Are Brand New to Sales?

One of the problems with having so many prospecting choices is knowing where or how to start. I wanted to devote this section to newer sales reps to help them get started. Please keep in mind, all you seasoned sales reps, this is for you, too!

Let's equate prospecting to golfing and let's look at the different golf clubs inside a golf bag. There are fourteen golf clubs, in a standard golf bag. There are twelve clubs, comprised of drivers, irons, wedges and a putter. Then there are two specialty clubs, such as a flop-wedge or lob-wedge. Those fourteen clubs allow a golfer to do their job better, which is to obtain the lowest possible score on the golf course.

Now if we use the golf analogy for sales, we can say there are fourteen different ways to prospect. A sales rep must use each one of those and needs to learn how to perfect using each one of those based on where they're at within their prospecting journey. This means they have to develop a cadence for what prospecting tools to use daily, what prospecting tools to use weekly, what prospecting tools to use monthly. Then develop a rhythm around it. Here are some ideas:

- Email
- Social
- Face-to-face
- Quarterly business reviews
- Networking events
- Community involvement
- Referral partners

The one skill you need to develop and develop well, is how you utilize the power of the phone. If this is something you fear or lack skillset in, then I suggest you find a good sales boot camp and learn how.

What's Next?

We've covered one skill you need to become a sales professional. In the next chapter, we will look at the next skill you'll need which is servant-led leadership. By changing how you lead, it changes your results. You will be surprised at what happens when you lead from the heart.

The right activity + enhancing the skill set + daily habits
= Sales Success

Chapter 5 Summary

- The reason why an empty pipeline exists is your fault. Not your company's fault or anyone else's. You need to make a non-negotiable deal with yourself, repeat to yourself every single day, "I must set aside the time to prospect."

- Nothing in your pipeline boils down to a few things: lack of practice, laziness, poor management and a reactive, instead of proactive approach to prospecting. Be Proactive.

- Sales management has blown it because they've fostered the behavior of inconsistently monitoring how all sales reps are prospecting.

- Face-to-face prospecting is not dead. It is still alive and well. The only difference is you adjust it according to the market.

- Online becomes an augmented prospecting approach based upon the social channels your clients and buyers hang out on. These social tools leveraged correctly, integrates strategically into a business development cadence.

- Social Window + Social Phone + Social Selling = Enhanced Sales Funnel

- The right activity + enhancing the skill set + daily habits = Sales Success

Chapter 6

Servant-Led Sales Leaderships

"Everybody can be great...because anybody can serve.
You don't have to have a college degree to serve.
You don't have to make your subject and verb agree
to serve. You only need a heart full of grace. A soul
generated by love."
Dr. Martin Luther King Jr.

George walked into his office distraught and extremely frustrated. Sitting down at his desk, the same old desk he'd been sitting at for well over twenty years, he gazed out the office window and questioned himself as to why new sales reps weren't seeking out his advice as much as they used to. Most of the time, he just brushed it off but something about today, got him questioning his worth.

Throughout his tenure, George had been the top sales rep, the big kahuna sales leader inside his company. He'd always been a natural at sales and had his sales bravado down to a science. Every sales rep was envious of him, and he was admired by all within his company, or so he thought. Because he was the top sales dog, bringing in truck-loads of money, he got away with many things others couldn't. Now the times were changing, and it was all due to Kevin.

Kevin started his sales career five years ago when he was in his late twenties. He was eager to learn and was diligent in asking George for his advice. He was always reading sales books and watching sales related training videos, all for his betterment. George would scoff and make fun of Kevin because in his mind, you either knew how to sell or you didn't. If you didn't know, then you weren't worth much of anything, and that's how George treated him. Some would say with a peasant's mindset.

Early on, Kevin's results weren't great, but he worked diligently, so the company kept him on the team. Everyone on the team loved Kevin because he was helpful, truly listened and shared his knowledge freely. As time passed, Kevin's results improved. Why? It became quite apparent, he served his clients rather than telling his clients what to do or taking them for granted. He led with his heart and not his wallet. This heartfelt servant message started to spread like wildfire out into the marketplace, and the business community sought out Kevin instead of George.

Sales reps inside Kevin's company began coming to him for advice. He treated them kindly and with the utmost of respect. Company managers started taking notice of Kevin and the amount of new business he was bringing in. Kevin was consistently on the phone or out in the community introducing himself, sharing with others his worth. He made prospecting and business development a non-negotiable daily activity. George, on the other hand, relied on his customer base, taking them for granted as he so proudly bragged about how well he was keeping them inline, almost with a bullying-type bravado. He hadn't produced a new customer in years and spent most of his time boasting to other sales reps about his past exploits.

It was this morning, the announcement of all announcements, the monthly sales reports and for the first time ever Kevin had risen to the top of the leaderboard, beating out George for the top spot. The room exploded in hand clapping, high-fiving, and cheers. George sunk into his chair with utter disbelief. How could this have happened? Kevin was a nobody!

The owner of the company stepped into his doorway. "George, I think we need to talk," as he closed the door behind him, sitting down directly across from George. By the end of the intense conversation, George agreed it was better to accept the retirement package they offered to him and leave with congratulations, than being let go in disgrace.

"How could things change so much?" George said to himself as he walked out of the company door for the last time . . .

Servant-Led Sales Leadership

No longer does old-school bravado and a bragging mindset work in today's sales climate. No one gives a rip what you've accomplished in your sales career. They want to know how much you care about them.

This is where I strongly believe servant-led leadership comes in, learning how to serve with heartfelt sincerity instead of learning how to service.

All too often in sales, we talk loosely about customer service. We talk about servicing the account or servicing the client. So much emphasis is placed on service as opposed to learning how to serve. To serve is to lead with the heart. It's the core of who you are. It's at the core essence of our existence, a heartbeat! It's treating people the exact same way you expect to be addressed. It's taking who you are as an authentic, genuine person and humanizing the entire buying journey.

It's about giving a rip about yourself, your career, your client, their needs and humanizing it. Often, we dehumanize the buyer's journey or the sales process as we make it all about us. Most look through their sales glasses as they smash through the mission as fast as possible to fit into a tight window of time, known as the thirty-day window. The time is now to change this behavior. It needs to become about the client, their needs, their wants and their desires.

To me, the art of serving is not manipulative. It's genuinely caring about somebody and their company. In your heart of hearts, you're there to help them do better business.

You must be able to lead with a helping hand. We have two hands, and in sales, one is used to shake someone's hand, and the other is used to lend a helping hand. Leading with a servant mindset means you genuinely care about helping the other person.

Adopting a servant leadership mindset takes a conscious effort by learning and committing to develop self-effectiveness in areas such as:

- Listening
- Empathy
- Healing
- Persuasion
- Foresight

Think about stewardship with your clients and prospects. Make the commitment to genuinely grow relationships, and with a sincere heart build a great community of clients.

Servant sales leadership is a journey. It is conducive to sales reps with a grit and growth mindset.

It's a Whole New World

Actions speak louder than words when serving with the heart.

Buyers today have been burned countless times because salespeople, sales leaders, and sales organizations make it all about themselves. This is one primary reason why sales teams and sales reps are struggling. Most will undeniably say they're customer focused or customer-centric, but do they truly mean it?

Are these merely words or is one living the true meaning of those words? It's interesting to peel back a company's mission statement or their value statement. They all have some kind of customer first philosophy, as they place the customer at the forefront, but when push comes to shove is there any substance behind the words, any meat on the bones, any action behind the verbiage?

In a YouTube video with Gary Vaynerchuk, he referred to sales in an offensive and defensive manner. Customer service is the defensive part of what we do as sales reps. When something happens inside the client-base, we have to assure them it will get fixed.

> ## Serving a client goes beyond actually doing what you've been hired to do.

The real question becomes, "What are we doing in the offensive mode to fertilize, nourish and grow that client experience?" This is the missing link. What are you doing to create a positive experience with the people who have trusted in you to do business with them? They've given to you and your company their hard-earned corporate dollars in turn for you to help them solve a business problem. It's not just handing over hard-earned money to solve a problem and then move on to the next corporate sales conquest.

We must enhance the experience. When you are truly genuine you lead with the heart. You're there to create a better experience, one that your customers never had before. This is what's it's all about.

Those that lead with the heart seek out authentic and genuine ways to continually serve those that mean the most to them—their clients!

On a consistent basis, they look their client's right in the eyes and sincerely thank them for their business.

Seek to Open Up Conversations

If you truly want to get to know your clients and prospects then take the sales hat off, roll up your sleeves and engage in healthy conversation.

Here lies the concern . . .

*How many sales reps have meaningful conversations
with their clients outside of the selling process?*

The best of the best know how to bring conversation out in the open. It is about uncovering the conversation your client or prospect is having with themselves. This enables open and honest communication to what is really going on providing the freedom to engage in a mutually beneficial relationship.

If your clients don't feel like they're being heard or understood, they may withhold critical information as to where they really are within their buying decision, which may diminish or eliminate your ability to impact the outcome.

Develop conversations, not sales campaigns. It is not about your agenda; it is about opening up a human to human conversation. It is not about you; it is about helping them. Develop a sincere desire and demonstrate you are interested in their world and what motivates them. They can smell insincerity and commission breath a mile away!

Customers have developed the mindset and expect that sooner or later they're going to be let down. They repeat to themselves often, "It's happened to us with the plethora of other sales reps that have come in here before. They all say great things, but then thirty days later something happens, or the first problem occurs…" The first problem is your big test. How are you going to handle the first problem that happens? Are you going to deal with it in a heartfelt manner or disappear or better yet start the excuse train to nowhere?

One of My First Experiences

One day, many years ago, I had an "a-ha" moment. I realized a good portion of my client base were non-profit organizations. I gravitated toward them, as I understood what they were going through. I sat on numerous not-for-profit boards and understood the issues and challenges many of them faced. More importantly, I knew they had to be sensitive with the dollars they spent.

My goal was simple, to help them become better stewards of their donor dollars.

I want to give a shout out in this book to an organization that is near and dear to my heart, Joni and Friends. You can find out more about them at www.joniandfriends.org. An absolutely fantastic organization led by Joni Eareckson Tada. She became a quadriplegic at seventeen when she was involved in a diving accident.

Joni and Friends is a Christian-based ministry located fifteen minutes from where I live. I didn't really understand the full degree what it meant to lead with the heart and to become a servant leader until I really started to gain a true understanding of the work behind Joni and Friends. Their core essence is to minister to those who are affected with disabilities all around the world.

A servant-led sales professional becomes a minister to those affected by dishonest and scrupulous sales reps.

I found this organization from a cold call some twenty-five years ago, and over time they became a client. They took the words of Jesus to heart in Mark 10:45, where He says,

For even the Son of Man did not come to be served, but to serve, and to give his life as a ransom for many.

And it became their philosophy. You have to lead with the heart, and you have to be a servant leader to work inside Joni and Friends.

This is where I truly learned how to give back. I became friends with their Chief Financial Officer, Billy Burnett, who is now retired and Charles McPadden, their IT Manager. They shared with me how to lead with the heart. We made it our mission to develop a genuine, authentic relationship. I observed what they did—their beliefs, even though our religious beliefs might have been different, I truly understood what it meant to give back by gaining firsthand experience of what they do with people who are wheelchair bound across the world.

There was something about this organization that touched my heart and dramatically changed how I dealt with my customers. From my first encounter, I told myself, "This is how I am going to treat every single account; I must lead and serve my clients with my heart. I must be true, stay genuine and with conviction be of help to them in solving their business problems, and challenges to the best of my ability." This became my pledge of allegiance. I became a true servant to my clients.

When I wrote my first blog post on leading with the heart, I got an email from Charles McPadden, stating he enjoyed reading it, "Hey, we have to go out to lunch."

So, I took Charles out to lunch. While we were eating, he shared with me something I will never forget, "You know, Larry, for twenty-something years you served our account with the utmost of professionalism. Every time you walked into Joni and Friends, you weren't there to sell me something. You were there to truly build a relationship with me, and you wanted to help. However, I knew when the point in time came where you had to put your sales hat on, I respected you for it because you had to earn a living and you led with your heart."

It was through those experiences that I learned how to put my sales hat on in a gentle way. I didn't become a different person. I was still the same person, it was just a mental shift in focus.

If you want to understand completely what it means to be a servant leader, you must be willing to give of your time. You have to give your time to those that need you the most.

That might be, you give more of your time to your kids or more toward your spouse, as you help them. More importantly, I think if you can become a servant out in your community, you will grasp quickly what it means to give back. It doesn't have to be much time; it could be an hour of your time, once a week. I encourage you to learn how to volunteer your time, which leads to the next section.

How Community Service Can Enhance Your Sales

"The best way to find yourself is to lose yourself in the service of others."
Gandhi

Community service allows those who participate to reflect on the difference they're making in society. Volunteering within the community teaches people of all ages and backgrounds compassion and understanding. People tend to gain the most from their community service projects when they volunteer their time to help people they've never connected with before. This interaction allows them to see life from a different perspective; re-evaluating their opinions of others.

The art of the help, isn't this the core essence of sales?

Is it helping our clients do better business? It's supporting those around us become better human beings. It's helping our friends, our family, and our network by lending a helping hand.

What does community service mean to you? For some, community service means helping inside a four-block radius of where they live. For others, community service means becoming active within their entire community, city, or town. Regardless of how you define community service, you can play an active role in building and helping it to grow.

Intangible benefits such as personal pride, self-satisfaction, and accomplishment are worthwhile reasons to serve. When you give back your time and talents, you:

- Solve community problems
- Strengthen communities
- Improve the lives of others
- Connect to others
- Transform your own life

How It Helps with Sales

Acronyms are a part of everyday sales communication.

- ABC: Always be closing
- CTA: Call to action
- ABP: Always be prospecting
- AFTO: Ask for the order
- FUD: Fear, uncertainty, doubt

Allow **ABH (Always be Helping)** to become one acronym you commit to doing weekly. This single act of kindness will propel your sales success and resuscitate your sales funnel, guaranteed!

I can't think of a more rewarding experience than lending a helping hand. Get involved and become active. By giving back, I've personally gained so much in return.

My personal commitment to help has led me to become active with my local Elks Lodge, Kiwanis Group and Senior Concerns; where I deliver food to home-bound seniors. My commitment to service led me to be awarded "Kiwanian of the Year, 2015" within my local community. This passion for service has led me to become president of my local Kiwanis club, 2017–2018.

My motto: Offer to help without expecting anything in return!

Always Be Helping: This Mindset Grows Sales

Rapport building during the buyer's journey is critical. Let's take your LinkedIn profile as an example, you can share and promote your volunteer experience and the organizations you support. What a great way to kick-start a meaningful conversation, as the buyer may share the same philanthropic characteristics as you.

Here's a great example. A huge shout out to my dear friend, Scott MacGregor, of SomethingNew. He is doing incredible, heartfelt service through SomethingGood. They believe good business starts with doing good things. They enthusiastically promote and financially support charities throughout the New York City region. In addition, their entire company devotes a full day every April during National Volunteer Week to give back to worthy causes. What's even more impressive is Scott self-funded a series of books titled *Standing O*—and all proceeds go right back to charity.

Now isn't this something to rally around?

Corporations Support the Community

Philanthropic efforts in supporting the community through 'giving back' sits within the core and mission of most corporations. Corporations embrace and make it their responsibility to be a leading corporate citizen. They look for diverse perspectives to inform the community, strive to strengthen through financial contributions and to become proactive in caring, all for the betterment of the community.

Here's a tip when it comes to prospecting: look at your target list of accounts and start conducting research. Look for the charities they support, the schools they support, or even the local events inside the community they volunteer within.

Get involved and volunteer, as you may never know who you will run into. These events will lead to meeting new people, starting new relationships but more importantly, you're starting new conversations.

Executives Sit On Not-For-Profit Boards

Quite often corporate executives, key decision-makers or even influencers as part of their civic duty will lend their insight by joining not-for-profit boards.

Join a not-for-profit board to elevate your status within the community. Find an opportunity within your community to lend a hand and give back. What a great way to offer your insight as well as your knowledge. You never know who may be sitting next to you during a board meeting.

Add not-for-profit organizations to your prospecting efforts. If you don't get involved, then think of all the board of directors you have the opportunity to get to know if these organizations become your clients.

Where to Start Your Servant-Led Sales Leadership Journey?

It's all about the activities to me. I want you to start thinking about what activities you can do to position yourself differently in the minds of your clients, buyers or prospects.

One way to do this is to understand the client's needs on a profound level. This means you must make a personal commitment to yourself that you must understand your client inside and out. Not just on a superficial level but on a real-deal level, a heartfelt level.

You must put your clients' perspectives and needs far ahead of your own to give yourself a fighting chance. Putting them first is not complicated. It's about making them feel important and valued. If they need help, there should be absolutely no hesitation. If there is a question, every effort should be made to answer it. If there is a complaint, every attempt should be made to rectify the problem immediately. Client satisfaction should be at the forefront in any reasonable situation.

Instead of worrying about being interesting, we need first to be interested. Develop empathy for your clients. Start to gain an understanding of what motivates them and how this can align with what you can deliver.

Your clients come first, no matter what. No ifs, ands, or buts! This is the only way of doing business and living the sales life. If you take care of your clients, they will take care of you.

You must help them to identify emerging needs. You must have your clients' best interests—which means you have to be continually educating them. This means bringing issues to the table that they have not yet realized.

And this is tough! The only way to do this is to immerse yourself in their business. You have to truly understand as you look for potential red flags within their company. When you uncover those potential red flags, bring a solution not yet noticed and remove the potential roadblocks.

Another action is continually being full of ideas and solutions. Bring alternatives into their business. Help bring to light some new business opportunities. Think about how you can help them do better business.

If you really want to take this to the next level, start taking some of your clients and other sales reps you may know and begin bridging people together. Start bringing your inner circle into their places of business to help them do better business.

We all know salespeople sell a specific suite of solutions based upon whatever their company's offerings are, but we also know those same businesses buy from other sales reps, they have different needs you might not be able to help them with, but you may know who can help.

Someone who's authentic, who's there to lead, and is there to help their clients do better businesses is going to bring in their inner circle, their centers of influence. They will connect them with the other clients they know that can help them do even better business. This is truly leading with the heart.

Be proactive, not reactive inside your client base. Don't be threatened that you might lose business in the process, because you won't. Don't be afraid that maybe the other person or company might take business away from you.

One More Thing

When you lead with the heart, it will always come back to you. Sometimes in sales, sometimes in referrals, sometimes in personal and business recommendations. When you do good, people notice. Conversely, they also notice when you don't meet their needs, and trust me, they can be very vocal about it.

In today's social business climate and with the advent of social media, it is very easy for someone to blast out their feelings about you on their social channels. It takes just a few seconds and boom your reputation is tarnished. It only takes the right person who's very influential to get upset with you because you didn't do what you said you were going to do. You didn't lead with the heart and broke their heart, now it's all over social media.

Is the process longer when we sell with the heart? It can be, but it's worth it in the end because you will build a clientele that will always be faithful to you and recommend you to everyone they know. This is when you know you've done it right.

Win the War and Their Hearts

In a business world where sales reps are viewed with negativity, an authentic, real-deal approach is a breath of fresh air. It may result in losing a few battles, but those who put their hearts and clients first are guaranteed to win the war.

- A servant sales rep has an authentic desire to serve
- A servant sales rep is all in
- A servant sales rep is focused on serving the needs of the person sitting in front of them

Whoever wants to become a sales professional must become a *servant*!

On our *Selling from the Heart* podcast, www.sellingfromthe-heart.net, Darrell Amy and I speak to the growing community of sales reps who are genuine, are the real deal, do the hard work and speak from the heart. Please take this to heart as you grow your career!

Case Study: H. Spaight

Honesty is not always easy when it comes to looking in the mirror. Prior to meeting Larry on LinkedIn in 2015, I felt like I had arrived, so to speak, and was who I wanted to be. Little did I realize that there was much more in store for me in the way of change.

I did not "buy in" to Larry early on. However, we had periodic conversations, and what Larry was cooking started to permeate and sink in. I started to realize that I was not current or truly relevant regarding today's approach to selling and leading. I was not bringing tons of value to my team or clients. The funny thing is that I thought I was bringing value to them.

After two years of back and forth, and tons of messages and article shares from Larry, I decided to hire him to help our sales team and me to modernize or, as he would say, to "future proof" ourselves to be relevant. This was before the release of *Selling from the Heart.*

I thought that this would be relatively easy. He would help me to become better on LinkedIn and that was going to help me to be more successful.

As the day began, Larry first asked about why. I thought I knew that already, but I really only knew what and how. Naturally, that led me to reading Simon Sinek's book, Start with Why.

If you don't know Larry, he not only writes articles every week and posts daily, he also is quite the reader. He has shared numerous articles with me, and still does by the way. He always found something that would help me in my journey to becoming a better leader.

After finally getting past my why, it brought clarity to what I am all about. Next, he helped me to drive stronger conversations, including the better use of questions. I had fallen into laziness when it came to conversations and, honestly, I was not really reaching or connecting with people the way I wanted to.

The ability to have deeper conversations opened the door for improved relationships, not only in business but personal ones as well. Simple questions were now exchanged for more sincere ones that showed I cared. The better conversational skills that I was developing were well received. I started seeing my relationships grow stronger.

As a side bar, my marriage improved, even after thirty years, based on the Larry Levine factor in my life. So too have the relationships with my children. The superficial comments and lame "How's it going?" questions were lazy and without emotion. No wonder my relationships had fallen a bit flat.

Many years ago, I read a verse that said, "Iron sharpens iron, so a friend sharpens a friend." I needed some real iron in my life. I was not as sharp as I once was, and I was reaching an age when people start thinking of winding down in business, not necessarily reinventing or repositioning themselves.

My background before I was in sales was the ministry. I served others. I was involved in mission work in foreign countries and I knew quite a bit about listening skills and self-awareness. However, these skills can wane over time without a little occasional reminder to improve them.

Larry is a big believer in community involvement, and I felt like those days of serving others were to remain in my past. I even started to rethink this viewpoint. I'm happiest in life when helping others and contributing. This led me to revisiting the world of helping others and becoming more active in that space.

For me, Larry has become a real friend. He has gone way beyond what I had originally hired him for. He has asked me heartfelt questions that really stirred my thinking. He often says, "You know I have mad love for you, dude," then hits me in the forehead with a question that would make me think like I never have before, at least not in recent memory!

As I look at the next several years on the horizon, I know that I have a real advocate and helper with Larry in my life. There isn't anything that I could not approach him for advice. In sales, we reach that trusted advisor state after years of showing we care and we are bright enough to offer advice when called upon.

Larry is my trusted advisor because I know he truly has my best interests in his heart. Thus, I was and continue to be "sold" on Larry and I am buying what he's cooking!

Chapter 6 Summary

- Servant-led leadership is learning how to serve with heartfelt sincerity instead of learning how to service.
- Adopting a servant leadership mindset takes a conscious effort by learning and committing to develop self-effectiveness in areas such as:
  o Listening
  o Empathy
  o Healing
  o Persuasion
  o Foresight
- Seek to open up communications.
- Use community service to enhance your sales.
- Understand the client's needs on a profound level. This means you must make a personal commitment to yourself to understand your client inside and out. Not just on a superficial level but on a real deal level, a heartfelt level.
- Is the process longer when we sell with the heart? It can be, but it's worth it in the end because you will build a clientele that will always be faithful to you and recommend you to everyone they know.

Chapter 7

Taking Care of Your Clients

*"Know your promise to the consumer
and deliver on it, no matter what."*
Shep Hyken

Slightly hunched over with his head down and shoulders drooping, Charlie slowly walked back to his cubicle after just receiving his third verbal warning this year from his sales manager. This time, the message was loud and clear, "If you lose one more current account, there will be severe consequences, and you'll not like the outcome!"

Freaking out, Charlie strolled into the lunchroom, poured himself a black coffee trying to settle his nerves. If there was a bottle of Jamison nearby, one could only imagine. He couldn't believe it. He thought Advanced Motion, Inc. would be his client forever. "How could Laser Technologies get one over on me?" Charlie knew his prices were competitive within the marketplace.

What else could anyone or another company offer that would sway them to take their business elsewhere?

Hurrying back to his desk, Charlie logged into his CRM, looked up the phone number of his contact, dialed and shockingly found out his main contact left months ago. Now Charlie was stuck, frustrated and pissed at himself. He didn't know anyone else in the company. Charlie knew if he attempted to call the new decision-maker, he would look desperate and embarrassed. This was all on him. The fault and shame was on him!

Charlie knew he had to do something quickly. What was worse, his sales funnel looked like the Sahara Desert—dry to the bone.

It's Not Just One Person Anymore

Back in 2016, CEB (Corporate Executive Board) conducted a survey of 14,000 mid-size businesses. Within this survey, one significant number stood out, 6.8. They uncovered that on average there were 6.8 people involved in the average B2B buying journey.

Hey, Charlie, what could have happened if you knew at least six people inside of Advanced Motion, Inc.? Would the outcome have been any different?

The number 6.8 got me thinking... I encourage all sales professionals to get intimately acquainted with at least six people inside every single one of your accounts. No, not in holy matrimony terms, but I'm sure you can smell what I'm cooking. Upper, mid and lower level management... You must build rock-solid relationships that spider throughout your client's office environment. It is these people that now hold the success key and affect the buying journey.

If you only know one or two people inside every account, you sit vulnerable to a possible hostile takeover. You run the risk and become susceptible to having somebody else build relationships inside your accounts. We all know who these people are, it's your competition! In this highly networked and digital business world, if you only know a couple of people inside your client base, you're a sitting duck! What's preventing you from building new and credible relationships with your clients?

I urge salespeople, you owe it to yourself and your company to build credible relationships with your clients. The bigger the fortress both face-to-face and online, the better. In so doing, you'll lessen the risk of losing them.

I could share story after story of sales reps who confidently strut around saying they have great relationships with their clients. "Don't worry, these people aren't going anywhere!" Until you peel the relationship curtain back and you find out the relationship sits with the person who signed the sales agreement, and possibly one or two other people.

There's a sickness running rampant inside most sales teams, and it's called complacency. Year after year, sales reps sit back, resting on their laurels, brainwashing themselves into believing their clients aren't going anywhere. What has been done to nourish and grow the relationships?

Before one knows it, their clients become vanishing acts just like magic shows in Las Vegas.

Unfortunately, I see and hear about it all the time. In a recent visit with a sales team, I stressed the point of how we need to build effective and credible relationships with more than just a few people inside every single current account (wide and deep), one of the Executive Vice Presidents of Sales said, "You know it's happened to all of us. We get complacent with the relationship, and suddenly the account looks elsewhere."

Let me share an example from my own sales career. This one packs a powerful punch! My largest account was a hospital. I was proud to have them as a client as it took me almost two years to secure. With extreme discipline, I conducted on-site assessments, built credible personal relationships with every major department; really understanding the issues and challenges they faced. By the time it was said and done, the head of facilities and the vice president of operations stated, "You know something, you know more about what's going on inside our hospital than our current vendor, and (b) some of our own employees."

It was 2010, and at that time it was the largest deal I had secured as a sales professional. In 2013, I moved on with my career, and by 2016, the hospital had moved on as well. I know why it happened as I had built a considerable fan base inside the hospital. They failed to strengthen and develop credible relationships once I left.

You see, *Selling from the Heart* sales professionals don't make excuses. They just dive in and build a relationship fortress around each and every account. No questions asked! No complaining, no moaning. They find the time and make it happen.

I urge sales leaders and sales management to start thinking about not only do their salespeople need to strengthen and build relationships inside their current accounts, they as management must do the same. Nothing worse than a sales rep leaving and the sales manager going back to their client, "Unfortunately, so-and-so has just left our company," and the next words uttered are, "Who are you?" "I am the sales manager." "How long have you been there?" "Ten years?" "Really, then how come I don't know who the heck you are?"

This is what I want sales reps to realize and to start thinking about. The more people you know inside of your company accounts and how well they truly know you, the better. Not only from a sales perspective, but from a management and from an ownership perspective. You're all in this together!

It's all about the client experience. What are you doing to provide an outstanding client experience?

What the Average Sales Rep Does

Unfortunately, the only time the average sales rep will see one of their clients is when (a) there might be a problem that arises or (b) they do the proverbial, "Hey, I'm just stopping by to check in on things," or better yet, when they want to sell them something but haven't seen them in months. I know all of you know what I'm speaking about. No planned and proactive visits. No 'love' has been given as the "all about you" syndrome sets in with client management.

The average sales rep takes care of their accounts with a just 'winging it' approach as they check in on a periodic basis. There's no plan and certainly no personal accountability as far as what they're supposed to do. Once the deal is signed, they may be present through parts of the installation and implementation, then they are off like a rocket onto another conquest.

It may take sixty, ninety, or even 120 days to go back into their account. How can you effectively build any kind of a relationship with people if you fail to hold yourself accountable to a proactive plan? There's a crap-ton of average sales reps with ordinary relationships, as they fail to put together any kind of post-sale relationship building plan.

They build relationships up to the point where the sale culminates. Then the mental voice in their head chimes in, "Now they're my client. They aren't going anywhere for a while," and they fail to capitalize on the single best thing they can do which is nourish the relationship.

It is not always the sales rep's fault. Many of them have never been coached nor taught what to do. Whose fault could this be? I wonder.

The Human Part of Sales

> **If you don't care for your clients and provide them with an outstanding experience, I guarantee there's someone waiting in the wings to enhance the experience.**

This chapter will make you or break you. If you take your clients for granted, sit back, become complacent, fail to continually engage and build upon the relationship, you'll lose them. I guarantee it! Today, your clients are asking so much more of you than they ever have before. They are holding you to a higher degree of accountability.

If you fail to nourish and continually bring value, I flat guarantee somebody else will eagerly step right in. This is why those that lead with the heart and not the wallet will win in the long run.

You must lead with a servant mindset by bringing the human element back into sales. Make it about the customer. Continue to take them through the journey after the purchase. Salespeople discuss everything that leads up to the sale but a true sales professional shares what's going to happen after the sale.

This is what you can expect thirty days from now. This is what you can expect ninety days from now. This is what you will get on a consistent basis from me. This is my commitment, and this is what I will do to grow our relationship. This, my sales friends, is the missing link. All too many focus on everything up to the sale and they fail to share what's going to happen after the sale.

In my opinion, it's the post-sale where the magic happens. This was my secret sales sauce.

Looking them right in the eye and with conviction, "Allow me to share with you what's going to happen when you become my client. This is how I am going to grow and nurture this relationship on a monthly and quarterly basis. This is what you can expect from me. Not what you can expect from my company, not what you can expect from the departments within my company, this is what you will personally get from me. This is my personal commitment to you and what I'm going to do to ensure you've made the right decision in doing business with me."

There are very few salespeople willing to do this because most make it about themselves and not the client. Yes, it occasionally came back and bit me in the butt, but in the long run I knew that deep down inside my heart, I was going to develop great relationships with my clients. This was based on me being genuine, authentic and a real deal human. This is what salespeople must get back to. It's human-to-human, face-to-face and the eye-to-eye commitment you make to your clients. They deserve it, and you owe it to them.

How Sales Professionals Take Care of Their Clients

Sales professionals start by setting up a post-sale game plan that's mutually agreed upon between the client and themselves. In other words, let me share with you what's going to happen after you become a client of mine.

A sales professional conducts a post-sale interview on how everything went during the buying journey. Making sure they fulfilled and acted upon all the promises made up to the point of the sale.

Then, a sales professional shares what will happen next. This is what you can expect from me on a monthly and quarterly basis. This is how I am going to grow our relationship. This will be through the insights I will bring to your organization. There will be ongoing and continued education.

Sales professionals take it to the next level. You must make three promises:

Promise Number One: You must have consistent touch points with each contact inside every current account.

Due to decentralization within organizational structures, people may be distributed across different divisions within their company or even locations.

You must pledge and make a promise to develop relationships with at least six people inside each and every one of your current accounts. Each contact has a different agenda, motivation and preconception. If you fail to build a strong tie to any one of these people you could see important deals collapse, relationships lost and more importantly potential revenue loss.

You must make a promise to become client obsessed. It's about building relationships, referrals and revenue. You must always be looking for blind spots and potential red flags within your current accounts.

Promise Number Two: You must conduct monthly site visits.

You must become visible and valuable inside your accounts. Monthly site visits become a necessity as you build a fortress around your client base. You must diversify your relationships while establishing consistent communication patterns during these visits.

As these visits are conducted, engage in quick conversations with key contacts and stakeholders. Be on the lookout for potential opportunities and/or red flags, which can then be brought up in your quarterly business reviews.

Become massively curious about your clients during these visits. This opens up additional opportunities for engagement while potentially solving problems which otherwise may have gone overlooked.

You must become proactive and look for potential issues before they arise.

By becoming visible and valuable with your client base, problems never really become huge issues. Your clients will grow and learn what to expect from you. It becomes your opportunity to say thank you for doing business with me. These become opportunities to make sure the solution implemented is operating correctly. Why is this so important? It's all about building additional and credible relationships.

In this modern business world, everybody inside of an organization has a network. Everybody inside of an organization has a circle of influence. Everybody inside an organization has other friends, and they will share their story of you and how you're taking care of them.

Promise Number Three: You must conduct quarterly business reviews.

You must demonstrate on a strategic level top-of-mind awareness with your clients. No questions asked, you must consistently conduct quarterly business reviews designed to create engagement.

These reviews are critical because they will:

- Turn your relationship from vendor to partner
- Reinforce your value
- Review/set goals moving into the following quarters
- Establish a pulse (How am I doing?)
- Capture and reinforce successes
- Secure introductions into people your clients know (referral opportunities)

What if your customer is not local? In today's world, not everything is local, but with technology such as Skype, WhatsApp, or Zoom, it makes the impossible possible. With video technology, this allows you to still conduct quarterly business reviews. On a side note, you can make a plan to hold an annual visit, barring expenses and the time of the year.

Video technology is where it's at today. There's actually no excuse why you can't visit your clients. What prevents you from using new digital or video platforms? Or, for that matter, any other technology out there so that once a month, you coordinate a fifteen-minute Skype call. There really is no excuse.

Other Important Things to Do

Sales professionals must consistently bring value, they must always bring insights, and they must consistently build credible relationships. It's being proactive in sharing ideas. It's being proactive in providing education, and to me, this is how you fertilize the sale afterward.

We operate in a highly connected business world, where not only do we have to build those face-to-face relationships, but we must create them online as well. This means a sales professional must socially connect with their clients. This means they must connect to their networks.

They must continually educate them by creating a stream of information through their social platforms. This provides insight and education to help them do their job better, allowing the sales professional to stay top of mind to their clients continually.

One way to stay top of mind is to marry your online relationships with your offline contacts, especially so within your account base. We all know you can't see your clients on a daily basis, as you would never get your job done. But in a connected world, you will soon find out how you can stay top of mind through social networks.

I encourage you to set up routine, planned visits that are agreed upon. Your clients know that at a particular time during the month, you'll be in their office, and in a certain quarter, you'll be conducting quarterly business reviews. I encourage you to become a facilitator of knowledge. Become the consummate sales professional.

Understanding how to cultivate strong client relationships is the key to your success. Research has proven that established clients cost less to service and refer new clients more often, without incurring additional costs. I encourage you to focus on nurturing existing client relationships, look after your existing client base and nurture the heck out of them. Think about how they can help you grow your business in ways you might not have thought about before.

Here are a few ways you can nurture your client base to build stronger and more rewarding client relationships.

1. Build trust

Trust is mission critical to any long-term client relationship. Building trust is straightforward as it involves managing expectations, managing effective communication and delivering on what you promise. Consistency over time as it takes time to build up trust but takes seconds to break it. The goal is to lay out the foundation for client interactions where they feel comfortable enough to open up about their goals and trust you to work for them to the best of your ability; having their best interest at heart.

2. Provide strategic advice

The greatest way you can add value to your clients is to provide them with strategic, actionable advice going beyond the most obvious solutions. Whether it's saving them money on products, finding the best solution, or offering insights about changing laws that can impact their financial position, strategic advice shows clients you deliver true value and helps you in nurturing long-term, mutually beneficial relationships.

In the end, it's about delighting your clients. If you provide them with real assistance and real experiences to help them achieve their financial goals and more, they'll become advocates which could lead to referrals and continued business.

3. Show you are accountable

Gaining your client's confidence is to own their outcomes. Take responsibility and ownership. Show them you're acting in their best interests and are fully accountable for the results, outcomes, and impacts on those interests. Manage the expectations, be realistic about the possibilities and always communicate to them that you'll deliver as you promised. If you encounter any setbacks, update them immediately and continue managing their expectations in a clear, transparent manner. Never let their issues fester as they will not go away.

4. Thankfulness

Salespeople use holidays as their way to say "thank you" for continuing to do business with them. As an example, Thanksgiving rolls around, hey, I'm thankful for you doing business with me, and then they deliver something special touting their thanks.

Please don't get me wrong, I'm not busting on holidays and being a Scrooge, but let's think about it: why do most salespeople wait until toward the end of the year to say "thank you" for being their client?

We always find around major holidays that most salespeople and their organizations thank their clients for doing business with them. A sales professional who leads with the heart, who holds their clients in the utmost of importance, thanks them every single day of the year for doing business with them. They thank them on a continual basis and not just on special occasions.

You must be thankful for your clients every single day of the year. You must look for opportunities to say thank you on a consistent basis. To me, and I ask you to think about it, when you get down to Thanksgiving and Christmas, how many cards and baskets are businesses inundated with? I believe the true message gets lost.

I am not trying to be anti-holiday but when a thank you gift arrives on May 3rd. It has a much higher impact.

Think about what happens when appreciation happens on a consistent basis. Think about creating a thank you program for your clients. I thank you for doing business with me. I thank you for this, I thank you for that. Do it with sincerity, as opposed to the only time you say "thank you for doing business with me" is around the holiday season, when a thousand other thank you cards and a thousand other gift baskets, and a thousand other wine baskets, along with a thousand other boxes of chocolates are sitting on that person's desk.

Most sales reps do just the bare minimum and send thank you gifts at holidays, but to me, a servant-led sales professional leads with "thank you" all the time. Leads with "I appreciate the opportunity to serve." They let them know it, and they broadcast it out. To me, this is what will make more of an impact than doing the bare minimum, achieving lackluster responses.

If you want to become a sales professional, then you must rise above, and go above and beyond the call of duty. Because you have no job if you have no clients. You become unemployed.

It All Comes Down to Giving a Rip

No matter what you do in sales, if you don't give a rip, then you won't survive in the sales world. You must look at the entire process and how you serve your client.

If you would like to learn more about caring for your clients, I encourage you to check out my weekly podcast with Darrell Amy called *Selling from the Heart*, at www.sellingfromtheheart.net. Each week we look at different topics that affect sales professionals and how they can become the best sales professionals by being their genuine selves. It's free training that will take your sales to the next level.

Chapter 7 Summary

- All sales professionals should get intimately acquainted with at least six people inside every single one of their accounts.
- Unfortunately, the only time the average sales rep will see one of their clients is when (a) a problem has arisen, or (b) they do the proverbial, "Hey, I'm just stopping by to check in on things," or better yet, (c) when they want to sell them something but haven't seen their client in months.
- Sales professionals start by setting up a post-sale game plan that's mutually agreed upon between the client and themselves.
- Sales professionals make three promises:
  o Consistent touch points with each contact inside every current account.
  o Conduct monthly site visits
  o Conduct quarterly business reviews
- Other important things to do:
  o Build trust
  o Provide strategic advice
  o Show you are accountable
  o Thankfulness all the time

No matter what you do in sales, if you don't give a rip, then you won't survive in the sales world.

Chapter 8

Continuing Education

"Formal education will make you a living;
self-education will make you a fortune."
Jim Rohn

S tuart, reviewing his month-end sales report once again, shook his head in disbelief. It had been six plus months since Stuart hired Connor and the sales just weren't consistent month after month. Based on Connor's resume and his interview, Stuart expected Connor to be producing consistent results, but quite frankly the opposite was happening. His sales were lackluster at best. For someone with so much experience, so much talent, who portrayed himself as a professional, he was being outsold by much newer sales reps.

Stuart just couldn't figure out what was going on with Connor and decided he needed to speak with him. As he started strolling over toward his sales cubicle, he passed the break room and heard Connor's voice. Totally shocked, he overheard Connor bragging to someone from the admin department. With bravado, he was sharing how well he thought he was doing and how he'd soon be running the entire sales department.

Stuart wound his way right into the break room, and Connor guiltily jumped back, clearly hoping Stuart had not heard his last comment. "Connor, may I speak with you for a moment?" "Sure." Connor gestured a goodbye to his admin friend and followed Stuart into his office. "What can I do for you, boss?"

"I would like for you to explain and based solely on y reports, why have you ranked dead last again this month?" Without even flinching, Connor replied, "Well it's quite simple. I was helping out one of the newer reps with some of their deals. Don't worry about it, Stuey! Next month is my month, I promise you. Don't you worry about it."

Even though something was eating away at Stuart, he accepted what Connor said and left it alone. Over the next few weeks, he started to observe Connor carefully. He noticed that Connor spent quite a bit of time inside the office, talking to everyone except new, potential customers. When Stuart checked Connor's company phone usage online, much to Stuart's disappointment, there were more personal calls than business calls. There was not much action to lead him to believing Connor would bring in any new business.

A week before month-end, a young sales rep approached Stuart requesting his help. She shared with him that Connor had been badgering her for sales leads and had promised her that if she served up a few phone numbers to him, he would make sure she'd be "taken care of." The more she refused, the more Connor pressed, making her extremely uncomfortable.

Enough was enough. Stuart phoned the HR department to make a formal request to have Connor terminated. Glancing at his computer screen, he noticed an email from Connor informing him of his immediate resignation.

In it, he gave the following reasons for terminating his own employment:

- The company's sales process sucked as there was no way to assist salespeople in producing leads.
- The other salespeople were sabotaging him.
- He couldn't work for a company that wouldn't give him a chance to prove himself.

He didn't even give a two-week notice. He just plain old quit and walked out. Stuart, being a young and inexperienced sales manager, had never had to deal with this type of behavior before. Not sure what to do, he looked to confide in the vice president of sales. His boss smiled as Stuart shared the course of recent events. He nodded knowingly and said, "Quite simply, Stuart, you've been conned by a career job hopper. A sales retread: all talk, no action."

Every new manager has experienced these fools at least once. "Unfortunately, I bet you didn't do your due diligence, did you?" Stuart's boss asked him. "No, I didn't. I called one reference, and they gave Connor a glowing review." "Next time call the second, the third and completely peel it back. Get me involved as well."

Stuart learned a valuable lesson. The next time he interviewed someone who was all talk based upon success gone by, sounding great and looking good, he'd check all references, double- and triple-checking what needs to be done.

Sales Job Hopper Syndrome

A sales job hopper is somebody who relies on their past experience, their so-called successes to help them land yet another sales job. In the industry I grew up in, you'd see these people frequently, especially the tenured ones who ask for a guaranteed base salary until they get their 'feet situated' and a pipeline built; only to milk the pasture providing very little in return. I politely referred to these clowns as "career sales hoppers." They are sales reps who promise the world and give nothing in return. Most of the time they should have never been hired but they managed to B.S. their way through an inept interview process.

Sales job hoppers piss me off and give this profession a black eye. They're the ones failing to continue their education. They fail to do anything to advance their career. They may have the "gift of gab" (or should I say the gift of bullsh—) to help them land a job, but within the due time, they become exposed for being a weak salesperson, an empty suit. They're exposed for being inauthentic, ungenuine and not the real deal. Simply put, a relic from the past gone by. We all know what happened to dinosaurs, don't we?

Sales relics keep moving from one sales job to another, as they have no plan, haven't practiced in years, and haven't bothered to self-educate and become consummate sales professionals. They've done absolutely squat to enhance their career further. I guarantee they haven't read a book, they haven't been to a training class, nor have they confided in a mentor. It's tough to succeed in sales today without continuing your education.

Sales, It's Evolving All the Time

If you fail to educate yourself continually, the sales world will pass you by. It's like a school teacher who fails to educate themselves yet trying teach their students new curriculum.

I'm heavily involved with the Kiwanis group here in my community. Our club recently had the head of the county teachers' association as a guest speaker. A retired school teacher herself, she mentioned, "School teachers must learn and absorb ten times the amount of content than that of their students." I thought this was interesting. It's not that the teacher needs to know everything, but they must learn content around various topics as they never know from what angle a student may ask them a question. Teachers must be able to facilitate their students' knowledge.

How does this relate to salespeople? Salespeople must know ten times the content than that of the buyer. If you fail to continue your education, then in the buyer's mind, you're failing to bring the goods. This is one huge reason why buyers look on the internet and self-educate themselves. Very few sales reps actually lead with insights and educate the buyer on how to help them do their job better.

What the Average Sales Rep Does

Most sales reps earn a failing grade when it comes to educating themselves. They tend to rely at best on their company to educate them. If this doesn't happen, then what?

The question becomes, "How much are you investing in your sales success?"

Let me ask you this question . . . Please add up how much of your own money you've invested over the past year in your private sales education. How much of your own money did you spend to learn something new about sales to help you improve your performance and enhance your sales skill set? How many sales books did you purchase? How many did you read? Have you hired a mentor? Do you attend sales conferences? Do you enroll in online classes to learn more about how to sell to your clients and prospects?

If the total amount you personally invested in your own sales success doesn't equate to 1 percent of your year-to-date earnings in the past year, then I urge you to ask yourself a very pointed and direct question, "Am I really that serious about my sales career?"

Ask any sales rep what's the last great book they've read. Ask them what's the last great podcast they've listened to, or what article they have read that has helped them do their job better. I can hear the crickets now!

There is a plethora of reasons why sales reps are in such turmoil. When it's all said and done, it all comes back to this: what are you doing for yourself to help you do your job better? If you look at other professional careers, they must continually upgrade their skills through some kind of certification process. But what about salespeople?

Far too often, most in sales seem content waiting for their employers to provide some sort of formalized sales training a few times a year. This is a true mental "tick-box" approach to training. They believe it's solely their employer's responsibility to train them to master their sales craft. Unfortunately, nine times out of ten, this becomes a losing strategy. Sales is an entrepreneurial profession. It handsomely rewards those who take risks and those who have the discipline, drive, and determination to work on self-improvement constantly.

To give some benefit of the doubt to sales reps, it's not entirely their fault. On a side note, there are not many universities offering certification, but this is changing. When I started my sales career, there was no going to college to earn a degree in sales. Today, many sales reps are self-taught as they receive their degree from the "school of hard knocks."

You can hire a business coach, and you can hire a mentor. Your company can train you, or they may opt to send you to training sessions. Unfortunately, many sales reps are left holding the training bag in their own hand. It's called learning by doing.

Learning via ride-outs with a sales manager, learning through observation as you package it all together to succeed hopefully.

Question for you: would you invest $20.00 per month for the opportunity to boost your commissions by 25 percent? Or, how about the chance to earn an extra $3,000 per quarter? Simply put, I bet you would. This is the monthly price of fancy coffees from Starbucks. Breaking it down into smaller amounts, this is 90 cents per day!

Could you set aside and commit to one hour per week to read one sales book per month if you knew you would gain two new strategies and techniques to help you win more deals— thus earning more money? I know you would. Which raises the question, "Then why aren't you doing it?" One massive reason sales reps are struggling inside many sales departments all points back to a lack of a formalized, planned and consistent education program.

How Sales Professionals Deal with Education

A true sales professional takes pride in their profession. They step up to the plate and take learning seriously. Learning is a non-negotiable activity. They rise to the occasion. They invest in themselves.

> **If you can't invest in yourself, why would someone else invest in you?**

Sales professionals take the bull by the horns. They pay for themselves to attend training conferences. They take action for themselves. They hold themselves personally accountable for learning and development. They commit to learning the art behind sales.

They consistently purchase books, devouring every page. They listen to podcasts, especially *Selling from the Heart* podcast, at www.sellingfromtheheart.net. They seek out coaches and mentors. They consistently seek out other sales professionals for advice as they bring them into their learning circle.

I invested $10,000 of my own money and hired a business coach over ten years ago. I experienced firsthand what a coach could do for me. If it weren't for my coach, I wouldn't have gained an understanding of what it meant to brand myself in the world of social media. I wouldn't have understood what it took to drive traffic to my social media platforms. I wouldn't have understood what it meant to tell my story in a digital world.

One thing I urge all of you to consider: make the commitment to yourself to never stop learning.

Sales professionals make a commitment to themselves, their career, their employer, and their family. They do what is necessary to succeed and grow as a sales professional. This is the one difference between a sales rep and a sales professional.

Still to this day, I have mentors that I look up to. People who've already been there, done that, and I learn from them. No matter where you're at within your career, there will always be someone who has done more than you, who can show you the way.

If you want to be successful as a sales professional, then you must be willing to help your clients and prospects. You must educate, engage, and excite them into a conversation. To do this, you must consume information. You must bring learning to the forefront of what you do. This means every day, you must read a chapter of a book. Every day, you must listen to a podcast. Every day, you must read business articles. Every day, you must consume and inundate yourself with your industries content. You must know ten times more content than the person that you are selling to.

If not, face the wrath of the price hammer—just saying!

You must become a facilitator of knowledge. You must be able to help your clients and prospects solve their business problems and challenges. To do this, you must become the credible expert within your marketplace and industry. You must continually stay on top of your game, and the only way to do this is to place learning at the top of what you do. If you fail to learn consistently, you will fail to constantly grow.

What Makes Sales Professionals Successful?

Great salespeople do the same thing every day. They are purpose-driven. They focus on the success and happiness of their prospective and current clients. They see the business world through the eyes of the other party. They are naturally curious and love serving their clients.

Five things sales professionals do:

1. They hold themselves to a much higher standard.

Top sales professionals who consistently deliver outstanding results make high performance the de facto standard. They realize that the "buck" stops with them. They know their actions alone determine their outcomes and they do what's necessary to achieve their goals. They never blame internal problems, the economy, fierce competitors, or other factors if they fail to meet their sales quotas. With extreme self-discipline, they take it upon themselves as they self-manage to a higher standard as they fail to accept mediocrity.

2. They continually prospect, keeping their sales funnel full.

Top sales professionals divide their time between selling, prospecting and taking care of their clients. Top sales professionals, who crush their quotas, are fully dedicated to prospecting and have modernized their prospecting approaches to align with the modern buyer.

It's hard to sell something if you don't have a prospect to talk to. The most important part of selling is prospecting—finding new, qualified people to talk to.
Brian Tracy

3. They never stop learning.

Top sales professionals are always reading sales books, learning new skills, asking for coaching, and improving their own selling abilities. They never sit back and rest on their laurels. They are constantly striving and pushing themselves to improve. This strong work ethic pays off and results in sharper selling skills and improved win rates straight across the board. The most successful sales professionals are never content with their current abilities as they are continually learning and pushing their limits.

4. They are always helping.

Legacy, old school, and analog-minded sales reps are closers. The pitch starts the minute they open their mouth.

A *Selling from the Heart* professional places the customer's needs before their own. They develop trust with their prospects and clients. They leverage trust to gain a better understanding of their challenges, goals, and problems. Top sales professionals use their prospects and client's terminology to closely align themselves as to how they can help.

If a top sales professional believes the prospect or their client has the wrong goals, they don't hesitate to challenge them. They educate them as to why they may be wrong as they help their prospects and clients avoid potential business potholes or roadblocks.

5. They have become digitally savvy sales professionals.

In this highly networked business world, the Internet, along with Google has forever changed the sales process. In this modern buyer-driven society, sales reps must step up their sales game. They need to be viewed by their prospects and clients as trusted advisors.

Sales professionals must make the investment and commit to obtaining this status. Successful sales professionals invest the time to build up their online authority and presence. They read the blog posts their targeted prospects read, and they drive conversation around them. They follow them on Twitter and connect with them on LinkedIn, if applicable. They retweet their best messages and comment on their posted content. They join the same LinkedIn groups their prospects are involved with and answer relevant questions.

They become digital thought leaders and subject matter experts. They soon realize educational and relevant content drives online conversation, which ultimately turns into offline meetings.

Never Stop Learning

If you stop facilitating learning, if you're not putting education at the foremost of what you do, then how can you go out there and help your clients do better business? It's downright frightening, as we're already positioned behind the eight-ball in the sales world, especially in the minds of the buyer.

Can you imagine a real, genuine, self-educated, always-wanting-to-stay-on-top-of-their-game sales professional walking into somebody's office? Service exudes from their personality. It exudes from their pores, and the buyer senses it. "Finally, a sales professional has walked into my office as opposed to just another sales rep spewing self-serving, all about me, and my product information."

Develop yourself into the expert in your field

Sales professionals don't ACT as if they're experts. Sales professionals ARE experts. Customers will quickly sense if you're uncomfortable in your own skin, a beginner or full of you know what. To become an expert, you must excel at what you do; but to be excellent, you must practice, you must learn.

It is essential that you master the core fundamentals of your profession. This way, it becomes second nature to you and you become extremely confident when you're engaging with your clients and prospects. To become an expert, you need to discover your passion, your why.

- Why are you doing what you're doing?
- Why now?
- Why are you better than anyone else?

When you're able to answer these questions and clearly articulate it with confidence, then use this as jet fuel toward becoming an expert in your marketplace. Promote the value you offer your clients and prospects, as well as the possible problems you will solve for them.

Sales professionals are on top of their industry; they're always looking ahead and monitoring trends. They learn to master the short and long-term goals for their clients. Furthermore, sales professionals are keenly aware of their competitors. They know the competing products and services, how they're sold, whom they're sold to, and what, if any, potential gaps they can identify.

Make the Investment . . .

To become a sales professional a sales rep must invest their time and have enough patience to place learning upon a pedestal. They must remove the "I have no time," excuse and learn to have patience.

You must become patient in managing your own business expectations. Let's face it, selling can be tough. Patience helps you to remember what you do is difficult. The relationships you develop are essential to your success, and these are not created overnight. A true sales professional is tough and demanding on themselves.

Complacency stunts learning and development; it is a ruthless disease. It cares only to keep you weak and timid, keeping you in the "wait and see what happens" mindset. The hard reality behind this is while most sales reps operate with hints of contentedness, the top sales professionals inside your marketplace do not. With extreme precision, they have rewritten the playbook adapting to the changes inside the buyer's world.

Great sales professionals just don't appear out of nothing or nowhere. You're not born with the tools required to become a professional. You must train yourself. You must educate yourself. You must consistently hold yourself accountable to become the very best at what you do.

I want to encourage you never to stop growing. Become a sales professional who stays at the top of his/her game by making a commitment to learning and development.

Those who embody success believe in themselves. Do your best to have a positive mental attitude and a sense of control over your self-talk. This not only will help you to improve yourself from a knowledge standpoint, but it also helps you when it comes to your mind, heart, and soul.

This my friends, is what *Selling from the Heart* is all about.

Have you gotten your *Selling from the Heart* Self-Reflection Journal yet? If you haven't why not? This journal will help you apply what you have learned in this book and take your sales to a whole new level. Go to www.sellingfromtheheart.net/ journal and download yours for free right now!

Chapter 8 Summary

- Don't become a "sales hopper" who relies on their past experience, their past so-called successes to help them land yet another sales job.
- If you fail to educate yourself continually, the sales world will pass you by.
- Most sales reps earn a failing grade when it comes to educating themselves. They tend to rely at best on their company to train them.
- A true sales professional takes pride in their profession. They step up to the plate and take learning seriously. Learning is a non-negotiable activity. They rise to the occasion. They invest in themselves.
- Five things sales professionals do:

1. They hold themselves to a much higher standard
2. They continually prospect keeping their sales funnel full
3. They never stop learning
4. They are always helping
5. They have become digitally savvy sales professionals

If you stop facilitating learning if you're not putting education at the foremost of what you do, then how can you go out there and help your clients do better business?

Sales professionals don't ACT as if they're experts. Sales professionals ARE experts. Customers will quickly sense if you're uncomfortable in your own skin, a beginner, or full of crap.

To become an expert, you must become excellent at what you do; but to be excellent, you must practice, you must learn.

Content That Creates Conversations

"By creating and publishing remarkable content in the form that educates, informs, inspires and entertains, marketers can begin to build relationships with prospects early on in the buying cycle."
Jonathon Lister

athy walked into Kevin's office, plopped herself down on the empty chair inside Kevin's office. "You wanted to see me?" "Yes, I was speaking with your manager, and we were reviewing your sales results for the past quarter. I must admit, quite impressive." Cathy beamed. "Thanks."

"What's the secret and how have you been doing it?" Kevin inquired. "You probably won't believe me if I told you." Now Kevin's curiosity piqued. "I'm sure there's nothing you can say that would surprise me." "I post and leverage educational content on a few social media platforms, allowing me to drive additional business development conversations. This has helped me fill the top of my sales funnel." Kevin was floored. Social media was not the answer he was expecting. He was expecting to hear that Cathy had been getting out in the field, conducting more sales calls, participating in networking events, working more effectively on in-house leads.

Kevin, he's a sales veteran. He's been at the sale game for over thirty years and believes social media is useless for B2B sales, even LinkedIn. Aren't social media platforms used for posting jobs or looking for employees?

"I don't understand. How can you be driving business development on social platforms such as LinkedIn?" Kevin just had to know. Cathy proceeded to spend the next thirty minutes explaining to Kevin how she integrated the use of social media into her sales and business development process. Kevin just shook his head in utter disbelief. In all his years, he'd never heard of anything like this, but there was one thing he did know—results. Cathy was getting sales. As long as it continued, Kevin supported Cathy in doing it her way.

Content Is an Important Strategy for Building Sales in Today's World

As salespeople, we must learn to come to grips with the fact that we operate inside a digital business world. Everybody feels comfortable going to the internet, surfing to our heart's content as we absorb content online. We must come to realize that we live in an online world.

Salespeople can't go one day without hearing, "You have now entered the world of buyer empowerment." A special thank you goes to Google as buyers now can conduct research and make buying decisions independent of any form of communication with salespeople.

It's no secret, digital and online resources are playing a significant role in altering the way buyers buy. The landscape is changing rapidly as buyers conduct pre-purchase research to understand their options via a combination of channels. including search engines, social media platforms, email and numerous competitive websites.

A true sales professional learns how to digitally fish in the same online ocean that their clients and prospects educate themselves within.

Disconnected Alignment

Herein lies the disconnect . . . The way you sell and the way you buy are misaligned. Stop and think about it for a moment. When it comes to a major personal buying decision, I guarantee you take on the same traits as those of the buyers you are selling to . . . Are you starting to get it?

How Do You Buy Online?

Looking more closely at your own buying habits, you will soon discover that it's different than the way you sell. You're doing the same thing your buyer is doing.

You're going online. You start doing your own research. You educate yourself. You're looking for content to help you make a better decision. At some point in time, you will probably speak with a salesperson. You're in sales, and many of you hate speaking to your own kind. Folks, the businesses you're trying to help are doing the same thing to you.

A sales professional understands this reality and aligns their buying habits with their sales lives. A sales professional will serve up relevant, insightful and educational bite-size content to their clients and prospects to help them do business better. They make this a non-negotiable daily activity as they serve up content on a digital silver platter. This platter becomes the playground for a business development conversation.

I would like for you to internalize and visualize parts of your prospecting approach: think about how relevant and educational content can facilitate an online conversation with the modern, digitally driven B2B buyer.

A sales professional will integrate the use of content as an additional method of communication along with all their other outbound prospecting endeavors.

Build a Content Library to Stay Competitive

In cases where sales and marketing may not be aligned, a sales professional will take ownership by building a digital library of content which can then be used to teach and tailor their audience (prospects and clients) throughout the buying and sales journey.

A sales professional will become a librarian of knowledge. They source, read, learn and index this knowledge as they invite their clients and prospects into their den of insight.

Content As a Sales Positioning Tool

When I started down my social media path as a sales professional within metro Los Angeles, California, I had no content. I went on a digital fishing and hunting expedition, curating other people's content and I still do it today. This is how I educate my clients and prospects, so they can do better business. As a result,

I myself am learning. This helps to raise my business acumen, my knowledge and my position as a credible source of insight. I learn to speak the language of my clients and prospects based upon the content I consume.

How you Capture, Converse, Collaborate, and Connect along with providing relevant and insightful content to grab the attention of the executive buyer will determine your sales success in the twenty-first century.

Sales Reps Must Leverage Content As Bait

Where I really elevated my game, and where salespeople can really raise their game as well, is to start creating your own content. If you want to be seen as a credible expert in your field, you must begin to generate some of your own content. I know you have the time and I know that you have the skill set, it's a mind game, and you must overcome it. It starts with the dreaded "P" word that most in sales hate: *practice.*

I've personally written a blog a week since December of 2015. A special shout out to Keenan for the forty-five-minute conversation that inspired me to write every single week. I co-host my weekly *Selling from the Heart* podcast www.sellingfromtheheart.net with my close friend, Darrell Amy. Most importantly, I made the commitment to write this book.

I have sales reps, sales managers and even executives give me excuses as to why they can't write. I'm here to inform you, you can write. It's the same reason why most sales reps struggle when it comes to prospecting. Most of you hate prospecting because you fail to practice. It is the same reason why you hate writing; you fail to practice. Conversely, you will sit in front of your laptop for forty-five minutes constructing an email paragraph as to why somebody should meet with you. Isn't this writing?

A sales professional understands that writing content attracts prospects. I am here to inform all of you, wisdom often comes from the mouth of a sales professional.

Benjamin Franklin once said,

Either write something worth reading or do something worth writing about.

Salespeople have all the means to write content to help them build upon and expand their sales inside a digital business world. Just look at the number of weekly sales meetings you go on. It's these meetings that provide you a wealth of opportunity to capitalize on as you reposition yourself as the credible expert that I know you are.

Gather the top questions you hear from your clients and prospects during these meetings and answer them in a blog format. Potential prospects researching for those answers online could end up finding your blog posts.

Here are a few ideas for you:

- Top 5 Reasons Why Implementing Document Management is Critical to Your Business
- 3 Reasons Document Scanning
- Can Enhance Productivity Within The Accounting Department
- 3 Reasons Why Security Is Important Within The Digital Workforce

Your clients and prospects not only search by keywords but by topics or through questions entered into a search engine. If your posts are hitting on the issues your prospects are seeking, then you might start to attract potential opportunities and business conversations.

Take those questions being asked during your meetings and flip them into a 500-word blog post. Even if you feel you just can't write, if at the end of all of this you're still struggling, then I encourage you to speak into the recorder on your smartphone and get someone to edit it. If you're really adventurous, think about hiring a ghostwriter to write it for you. You have options.

What Social Media Platforms Should Salespeople Be Using?

No questions asked, no ifs, ands or buts, salespeople must have a professional appearance on LinkedIn. A sales professional leverages LinkedIn as their own personal website. It's a window into who they are. What makes them tick and what they're all about. They incorporate LinkedIn to help them articulate their values through the positioning of a well-authored story. They position themselves as a credible expert that people want to engage and do business with.

LinkedIn becomes a positioning tool. A sales professional identifies and learns to position themselves on the social platforms their clients and prospects hang out on.

If your buyers are on LinkedIn, then you must have a LinkedIn presence. If a vast majority of your buyers use Twitter, then you must have a Twitter presence. The same can be said for Facebook or Instagram.

As a sales professional within the office technology sector, I leveraged and integrated two social platforms: LinkedIn and Twitter. I poured myself into understanding how these two tools could help me drive sales opportunities, business conversations, and my sales funnel. I made this non-negotiable and held myself personally accountable to learn how to use them to the best of my ability.

I leveraged LinkedIn to position myself with credibility. This became my personal website, and I took pride in how well it looked. I knew firsthand my profile was better than 99.9 percent of my competition and used it as my secret sales weapon.

I positioned myself as a valuable resource as I educated, engaged and with excitement drove business conversations within my network. Throughout my LinkedIn profile, I had educational material for people to download along with personal recommendations and testimonials of how I helped my clients.

I encourage all of you to start looking to social media platforms to help catapult yourself to becoming visible and valuable to your clients and prospects. Start asking yourself, where do my clients and prospects hang out?

I found Twitter a great tool for social listening. I follow my clients. I target accounts by monitoring and listening to their tweets and retweets.

The top social media channels you should focus your attention on (in no particular order) would be LinkedIn, Twitter, Instagram, and Facebook.

One thing to note, it's hard to play on multiple social media platforms if you fail to comprehend the core foundation of one or two. Know how to position yourself on at least two social media platforms correctly. Know how to communicate and drive content on them as well. If you can't leverage two successfully, what makes you think you can manage three, four, or five with any level of success? Social media platform overload is a sure-fire death sentence!

The Different Types of Content You Should Use

Content personalizes the sales process. Conversations are personal, by nature. Unfortunately, most sales funnels aren't very personal. This may leave sales reps struggling to engage with prospects who may or may not know much about their brand and how they can help.

The only way to overcome any initial disconnect is through education. However, bombarding prospects with general marketing materials is not the answer; one-to-one personalization is. It's time to change the pace of sales by changing the way you sell. Sometimes just slowing down allows you to sell faster.

Sales is relationship building at scale. For some in sales, it may seem like a monumental task to spend quality time getting to know each prospect or customer personally, but a *Selling from the Heart* professional personalizes their approach integrating the use of content.

> **Content is for closers. So how are you aligning yourself with your clients and prospects during their buying journey?**

Let's be real, most prospects feel most sales reps are full of (insert your favorite expletive). As you capture, converse, collaborate and connect with your prospects, share with them your posts, educate and help them by guiding them in the right direction. Point them right toward your LinkedIn profile. This is where you promote your professional business brand, your story: how you've helped your clients and what your prospects can expect when they engage with you.

Think of all the collateral material you share with prospects and clients throughout the sales process. Each stage of the process demands educated conversations and a supply of relevant information. In this ultra-connected, instant-gratification, immediate -quest-to-search-out-information business climate, integrating the notions of content and collateral becomes a natural approach to help drive your value.

Google and the Internet have forever changed the sales process, the sales funnel, and the buyer's journey. In today's modern business world, engagement is one critical way you can keep your prospects and clients interested, educated, and committed to a lasting relationship with you and your brand.

As more and more people (prospects and clients) become involved in the buying process, it can become a long and winding business road.

Therefore, it's imperative . . .

- You must maximize every interaction with prospects and clients
- You must have a strong digital strategy
- You must make sure you have educational content for all stages of the buyer's journey

Sales professionals arm their prospects and clients with the right content at the right time, to help them make the best possible buying decision. Materials used correctly boost your brand, your trust, and your reputation, allowing you to become an educational source. Ultimately, this will elevate your position with your clients to the point where they become brand evangelists.

Content leads to conversations, Conversations lead to
meetings, Meetings become one step closer to a sale.
No conversations = No Sales!

There is a plethora of content out there you can use. It can be business-related content. It could be educational-related content. It could be inspirational, video or infographic content.

Salespeople are always asking me, "Where do I find content?" or "what kind of content do I post?" Here's some advice, go back to your clients and ask multiple people inside the company, this could be decision makers, influencers or even end-users, "What online sites do you use to educate yourself?" "What are your favorite go-to sites you frequent to help you to do your job better?" Everybody has them.

A chief financial officer may have their top two or three favorite sites. An IT manager may have their top two or three sites which are completely different. An office manager may have their top two or three sites, which are different again. Somebody in accounting will have the same. Are you starting to get it?

Why is this important? You must become aware of and learn about the sites they're educating themselves on and in turn, serve them up bite-size chunks of content to consume.

It's equally important to pay attention to the type of content you post depending on where you're at within the sales or buying journey.

The following will help paint the content picture...

Top of the Sales Funnel

Here, sales professionals are driving awareness and positioning themselves as credible resources. This could be . . .

- "How to" blog articles
- Infographics
- Content from credible resources, thought leaders or subject matter experts

Middle of the Funnel

This is where sales professionals connect with prospects through sharing information. This could be . . .

- Case studies
- Long form blog articles
- Relevant industry news
- Favorite books (*Selling from the Heart*)

Bottom of the Funnel

This is where sales professionals engage one-to-one with prospects. This could be . . .

- Long-form blog posts
- Customer testimonials
- Peer recommendations
- Visual media
- Case studies

Does Content Directly Create Sales?

No, content will not directly create sales, but content helps you to open up and drive a conversation. Content is fuel and nourishment to the sales process. We all know the sales process starts with a conversation and ends with a conversation. The content you use will help you down the sales path, culminating in you closing more sales.

Content Facilitates the Buying Process

In this highly digital and connected business world, everyone is quite comfortable going on the Internet to educate themselves. So, content must become part of the business equation for you. You need to become cognizant of how many pieces of content your clients and your prospects consume during their buying journey.

If you would like answers to the content question and how this correlates to your clients, then I urge you to go back to your clients and ask, "How many pieces of content, how many pieces of educational material and how many pieces of information do you consume during your buying journey?" Then pose the second part of the question, "At what point do you have a conversation with a salesperson about this content to help you make a buying decision?

How Do You Use Content to Create Conversations?

This is difficult for many in sales to grasp because I am frequently asked by sales reps, "How do I open up a conversation online?" If you struggle doing conversations face to face, you will struggle with opening up discussions online, and especially with content. I find many in sales overthink and complicate this way too much.

Content Facilitates Conversation

You must position yourself with the right tools to have conversations with your clients and prospects throughout each stage of their buying journey. Content is one tool enabling these conversations. Content attracts and draws in prospective conversations. Content educates prospects and may potentially help them solve a particular problem which in turn may steer them to a buying decision. Delivering valuable and educational content positions you as a relevant and useful source. Your prospects crave sales professionals who can have intelligent conversations and provide a helpful message.

Sales Professionals Learn How to Feed Their Prospects Cravings With Content and Conversations

One way to create a conversation with your content is to ask questions. Likes, comments, and shares are your ability as a sales professional to create a dialogue. If you don't do anything with likes, comments or shares, then you'll never open up a conversation.

You must become proactive! If somebody likes, comments or shares a social media posting it's your responsibility to say, "Thank you for enjoying the article I just posted, what were a few things you learned from it?" Or, thank them for commenting on it and continue the conversation.

It's no different than in the face-to-face world. If you're introduced to somebody, I guarantee you'll exchange a few pleasantries and might even further the conversation. Most won't even give it a second thought, but for some reason, many of you struggle with how to create a discussion online, and it's really no different.

I just love having conversations. I learned a long time ago, "just simply continue the conversation!" Whether I wrote the article, curated it, whether it's my podcast or I'm promoting somebody else's podcast, if somebody likes, comments and shares then it's my responsibility to engage back and drive the conversation proactively, with sincere intent to continue the conversation. This is no different than the face-to-face world we all live in.

If the conversation is positive and rewarding, I'm going to invite them to connect in a way that is more personal. "I am glad you've been enjoying my content," or "thank you for the comment on my last blog post. I am glad you found it insightful. It would be an honor if I could connect with you. Look forward to getting better acquainted."

Once you've connected with meaning, now is the time to get to know them, provide value to them and show them you're a credible expert within your industry. I might say, "Thank you for connecting with me. I'm here to be a resource to you. By the way here's the last episode of my podcast, I would love for you to listen to it and let me know what you think."

It Can Be Done

Creating conversation online is not difficult. You must be consistent with your actions and have patience. You must post content with consistency. You must acknowledge those who like and comment on your posts. You must personalize all connection requests. You must provide value and bring a sincere desire to help. You must invite them to take the conversation offline, where you can engage in a more personable manner.

If you want to sell in a digital world, then you need to learn how to drive a digital conversation. What a journey this has been and in the final chapter we will tie it all together.

I encourage you to check out the *Selling from the Heart* podcast, at www.sellingfromtheheart.net, where I teach you how to use social media to build your sales business. Self-education is one of the best things you can do for yourself. I get what you may be going through. I've walked a day in the life of your shoes. I have "been there, done that" and continue to eat what I preach. I can help you to avoid the pitfalls, because I have hit them all.

Case Study: J. Joy

Thank you, Larry Levine, for your labor of love called *Selling from the Heart*. This is a must read for every sales professional, whether you are a green pea to the sales industry or a veteran.

I remember the moment that I discovered Larry's book, *Selling from the Heart*; it felt as though it was written just for me. I knew that I was different because I truly care about my clients and wanted to make sure they knew I was there for them. When Larry wrote about being authentic, heartfelt communication, and getting rid of mediocrity, I knew that I finally found a kindred soul in the sales industry that dared to be different. Larry, I applaud you.

Being an avid reader and learner of sales, sales processes, sales leadership, prospecting, etc., *Selling from the Heart* is the only sales book that I read from cover to cover. All the rest were listened to on Audible. Here's a little secret: I actually have it in all three formats. Being so impressed with the content, I purchased and sent Larry's book as a gift for the CEO, Senior VP, and VP of sales for our company.

Selling from the Heart inspires you to truly become the best version of yourself. Larry helps you understand your personal brand, think about how you are perceived by your clients, and asks you thought-provoking questions on how dedicated you are to your career. He makes great suggestions on investing in yourself and keeping a positive mental attitude.

After reading *Selling from the Heart*, I led with more confidence knowing that there were many sales professionals out there helping others in the way that Larry not only writes about, but also emulates in his book. You are truly an inspiration. At one point in my life, I almost did not enter the sales profession because I saw so many empty suits or people acting like a used car salesperson. I did not want my reputation to be tarnished by such garbage. Larry, you have started a nationwide movement in every sales profession to put others ahead of yourself and, some day, children in school will say to their teacher, "When I grow up, I want to be in sales." Thank you for transforming the way people sell.

Hidden in this book are the keys to sales success. When I train new agents in the insurance industry, one of their first assignments is reading or listening to *Selling from the Heart*. It helps educate us about every aspect of the sales business, including marketing your value and uniqueness, overcoming rejection, ways to prospect, how community service can enhance your sales and, most importantly, to not reek of commission breath. Just a word of advice: clients can smell it a mile away.

In closing, I would like to give a huge heartfelt thank you to Larry for sharing his authentic self with the world. The impact that *Selling from the Heart* has made on the sales community will never be known in its entirety. I can say this with utmost confidence: with your book, you have given others like you and I a community to be a part of with like-minded sales professionals.

Jacqueline Joy-Ribak, Sales Leader, USHEALTH Advisors

Chapter 9 Summary

- As salespeople, we must learn to come to grips with the fact that we operate inside a digital, business world.

- The way you sell and the way you buy are misaligned. Stop and think about it for a moment? When it comes to a major personal buying decision, I guarantee you take on the same traits as that of the buyers you are selling to.

- In cases where sales and marketing may not be aligned, a sales professional will take ownership by building a digital library of content which can then be used to teach and tailor their audience (prospects and clients) throughout the buying and sales journey.

- How you Capture, Converse, Collaborate, and Connect along with providing relevant and insightful content to grab the attention of the executive buyer will determine your sales success in the 21st century.

- Salespeople have all the means to write content to help them build upon and expand their sales inside a digital business world. Just look at the number of weekly sales meetings you go on. It's these meetings that will provide you with a wealth of opportunity to capitalize on, as you reposition yourself as the credible expert that I know you are. Gather the top questions you hear from your clients and prospects during these meetings and answer them in a blog format. Potential prospects researching for those answers online could end up finding your blog posts.

- Salespeople are always asking me, "Where do I find content, or what kind of content do I post?" Here's some advice, go back to your clients and ask multiple people inside the company, this could be decision makers, influencers or even end-users, "What online sites do you use to educate yourself?" "What are your favorite go-to sites you frequent to help you to do your job better?" Everybody has them.

- Content will not directly create sales, but content helps you to open up and drive a conversation. Content is fuel and nourishment to the sales process.

- One way to create a conversation with your content is to ask questions. Likes, comments, and shares are your opening to create a dialogue. If you don't do anything with likes, comments or shares, then you'll never open up a conversation.

Chapter 10

No More Empty Suits!

"To be successful, you have to have your heart in your business and your business in your heart."

Thomas Watson, Sr.

Unfortunately, in the sales world today, there are a tremendous number of empty sales suits. The sales profession can do better than they're doing. The issue boils down to misalignment. Most in sales are misaligned with their inner self, which tends to lead to chaos. It's hard to become the best version of yourself if you have no clue or can't identify with who you are.

Your prospects are smart. Your clients are even more intelligent. They can smell commission breath a mile away.

Sales Professionals Don't Reek of Commission Breath

Commission breath is the ultimate sales buzz-kill. It ruins a sales meeting in seconds and plagues the offenders immensely.

Commission breath describes a sales rep who's so hungry for a deal that they will say or do anything just to get it. They crave commissions so badly that prospects smell it on their breath a mile away. They're a shark in a suit, circling around red sales meat!

These sales reps are constantly in beast mode. They're always on the prowl, hunting and lurking for any opportunity to pounce on a sale. Their modus operandi is quite clear . . . make a deal, grab their commission and move onto the next sales kill. They're more interested in the commission than the relationship.

Commission Breath Is a Foul Odor

Your clients are way too smart and can immediately smell commission breath. Showing up, spewing and spraying insincere sales jargon; reeking of commission breath will instantaneously kill a deal. Sales reps who start off a meeting talking about how great they are, stink up the business environment. Sales reps who push their services stink up the business environment. Sales reps who are self-centered, providing reason after reason why you need to do business with them stink up the business environment.

Curing Commission Breath

The dishonesty by these commission-breath sales reps has caused the sales profession to suffer collectively from disparaging names such as 'snake oil,' and the infamous 'used-car salesman.'

This can be cured by adopting a *Selling from the Heart* life-style. *Selling from the Heart* professionals genuinely care about their clients. They give a rip and love to serve as they help their clients get their best outcome.

Selling from the Heart sales professionals become absorbed with their clients' needs and not their own.

Selling from the Heart is not a fad. It's not a strategy. It's a way of life.

Just Be Yourself

All people want is for you to be the best possible version of yourself. There's an awful lot of sales facades out there, con-cealing a less-than-pleasant form of reality. All your clients and prospects crave is a normal, genuine sales professional who cares about them and wants to help them.

It is all about self-alignment. How well do you know what you're all about? Once aligned, you can then become better at prospecting, better at taking care of your current clients and more importantly, better at driving a business conversation.

I know this works. This is what I've committed to for almost five decades: the 1980s, the 1990s, the 2000s, the 2010s, and into the 2020s. People just want to know that you care. They want to know you genuinely have their best interests at heart. They want to see that you're there to help them to do better business. Commit to it. Live it. Walk it and talk it; if you con-tinually do this, you'll lead a successful life.

Within my sales career, I knew some salespeople who could outsell and outsmart me, but I knew no one would ever out-care me. There are too many salespeople today hiding behind tech-nology. There are too many keyboard sales warriors attempting to build business relationships. There are very few salespeople that can look somebody, dead square in the eye, and with conviction shake their hand and say, "I'm here to help. I truly care."

Sales Professionals Are Leaders, Not Empty Suits

Sales professionals are effective in opening up business conversations because they speak the language of leadership. This language clearly conveys their ideas to their audience. They use language which precisely explains their thinking to the hearts and minds of those whom they wish to move to action, their clients and prospects. Sales professionals are not empty suits in the eyes of their clients and prospects!

> **A sales professional is heartfelt, sincere, and fills out a suit with empathy, emotion, and excitement.**

A *Selling from the Heart* professional understands how to create and deliver their value proposition in a way that captures the heart and mindshare of their clients and prospects.

If you don't know the value you bring to your current clients, then how do you know the value you can bring to your potential clients? Sales professionals know the "why" behind their value proposition and use this to create heartfelt alignment with their clients and prospects.

The reason why prospects and, yes, sometimes clients view you as an "empty suit" as they pay lip service to you is that you haven't personally brought them into your value proposition. How well do your clients know your value proposition? It's about serving and delivering a measurable amount of value at all times. Live it, walk it, talk it and broadcast it for everyone to hear. This, my friends, is not an empty suit!

What's an Empty Suit?

According to the Urban Dictionary, an empty suit is someone puffed up with their own importance but having little effect on the lives of others. A true empty suit conjures up the image of a business suit of clothing without a person in it who really doesn't know what he or she is doing.

> **There are way too many sales reps out there who believe they are "A" players, but they are nothing more than "C" players hiding in an empty suit.**

How well are you demonstrating competence? An executive appearance, presence, and attitude may open some business doors of opportunity, however; without skill, those prospects can quickly dissipate.

An executive presence – Competence = An empty suit

What happens in the first meeting with a prospect, as they share their heartfelt problems and all you can add to the conversation is a stream of buzzwords, canned pitches, and sales jargon? In a split second, this becomes painfully obvious to them that you have no empathy, no clue about their concerns, issues or how you may even help to solve their problems. This, my friends, is an empty suit. You're dead in the water!

Heartfelt Professionals Wear an Authentic Suit

An authentic sales professional leads with the heart by becoming open and vulnerable. They absolutely understand their weaknesses and are extremely comfortable in their own skin. Sales professionals who lead from the heart have courage. The courage to be human in a sales world full of facades.

> **Trust yourself, let go of expectations, go for everything you've ever wanted, and stop living your sales life as never having tried.**

These professionals develop relationships to:
- Acknowledge the human aspect of sales
- Acknowledge they must know themselves first
- Acknowledge credible relationships are the core foundation

This, my friends, is an authentic business suit, not an empty business suit!

Don't Be Mediocre

Sales reps are mediocre because they are afraid to think big. A mediocre sales rep operates in a state of accepting and working according to average standards, in other words: just getting by; barely making it. Managing with mediocrity creates a mindset that living in the comfort zone is acceptable. Too many sales reps are comfortable living in mediocrity. They choose to follow in the footsteps taken by many other sales reps because they believe it provides a sense of security.

A common mindset prevents those from becoming the best version of themselves, the sales professional I know they could be. They settle by following other like-minded sales reps down the same mediocre sales road, terrified of taking the steps toward loftier sales goals.

You can survive and get by operating with a mediocre mindset, but you'll never thrive. You'll always be among the other "me too" sales reps. A "me too" sales rep follows the other "me too" sales reps, mirroring and mimicking their every move; just like the pied piper. This keeps them all average as they suffer in togetherness through the same problems afflicting the majority of today's sales teams.

Mediocrity Is Safe!

Taking a risk is scary. Within our sales lives, each one of us will face a risky decision. One can decide to take the chance, leading them down the road to betterment or avoid it and stay mediocre. When the time comes, many simply freeze, stopping dead in their tracks becoming afraid to go for what they desire, a better sales life.

It's the numbing of the mind that condemns one to a mediocre, boring life. Whenever you come across risk, search within your heart and go for it. This requires courage and resilience. Rest assured, you will survive and lead a fulfilling sales life.

Sell from the Heart and Wage a War against Mediocrity

There are millions of sales reps out there, yet few excel and become a sales professional. A *Selling from the Heart* professional takes the art of professional selling seriously. They study the profession. They read, learn and continuously grow; nurturing their mind knowing it pays off in the long run. They understand the road to success takes time and patience. They hold themselves accountable to never becoming mediocre.

> ## A vast majority of sales reps are mediocre and average at best.

Three truths you should know about a *Selling from the Heart* professional as they wage war against mediocre sales reps.

They Practice Their Selling Skills Like An Athlete

A *Selling from the Heart* professional practices for countless hours, just like a professional athlete. They understand that the process of developing their talents will have obstacles along the way. They embrace the challenge by getting better every day. They know failure is another challenge, a roadblock to overcome.

They consistently practice prospecting, networking, asking great questions, uncovering their value, presenting their value, advancing their career and most importantly serving their clients.

Top athletes encourage feedback from their coaches, using it to focus on areas of improvement. The same can be said for a heartfelt sales professional. A less successful sales rep will tend to dismiss, ignoring feedback and focus on the person providing it, rather than using it as an opportunity to reflect and grow. Does this sound all too familiar?

They Don't Chase the Shiny Silver Bullet to Success

No one single thing makes a great sales career, it's a bunch of little things done well, every single day. It's consistent prospecting, building a strategic network, gaining business knowledge, self-awareness, practicing the art of conversation and time management, to name a few.

> **A complacent mindset is a death sentence when it comes to learning.**

Stop looking for the one thing to propel you to greatness. Instead, focus on developing your personal and professional skills.

A heartfelt sales professional chases their potential with patience. They understand that their clients, their family, and their career desperately need the best version of themselves. Patience takes time and conscious effort to master. A professional understands impatience leads to their demise.

They Seek to Serve, Not to Be Served

The highest calling for a *Selling from the Heart* professional is to serve others. They understand serving the interests of others by helping them overcome challenges to achieve their goals is a satisfying way to live their sales life.

Life is truly lived through moments of service to our fellow human beings. These individuals find absolute joy and contentment in serving their clients.

- Servants seek to make themselves available to serve.
- Servants seek to pay attention to others' needs.

- Servants seek to do every task with equal dedication.
- Seek to be "great"; if you want to be "successful," learn to become a servant.

Stop selling . . . start serving . . . start being a leader of yourself.

Let's Call a Truce and Put an End to Mediocrity

A mediocre sales rep easily gives up in their quest to become a heartfelt sales professional. Why do they do this? It's because pursuing this lifestyle is lonely, hard work and often goes against the general opinions shared by other sales reps.

Being mediocre is the classic "stick or twist." Are you going to hold on to what you have or take the gamble in search of more? All too often, sales reps stick with what they know, because it's safe. "The reason mediocrity is worse than failure is very simple," says HubSpot founder Dharmesh Shah. "Failure lets you move on, mediocrity stalls you and keeps you from reaching your potential."

Success is exciting and so is failure. Mediocrity? Well, that's a decision only you can make!

You Must Keep Learning!

There are way too many sales reps that have stopped learning. What's even worse are the tenured sales reps. Tenured reps have built up the mindset of "been there done that" and have just stopped learning because nobody is challenging them to become better.

Management is not challenging them, ownership is not challenging them and not even other sales reps.

I was amongst a group of peers, and someone had thrown out the question, "What sport reminds you of sales?" knowing I'm a complete sports junkie.

I said, "You all are going to hate me for this, but there's not a single sport out there that reminds me of sales."

The group almost wailed in unison,

"Why?" I replied, "Because to compare sports to sales, I ask you to consider and answer the following: how many managers and leaders are holding their teams accountable to practice, prepare, and plan every single day when they come to work? How many managers or leaders are role-playing, studying game-tape with their team? How many of them are observing and breaking down the work done by their sales team? How many managers or leaders are out there who actually require their team to practice on a daily basis?" Only a few.

You see, this is the scary part. Until you can answer these questions, then you can't compare sports to sales. Until you can get the core fundamentals down that sports athletes are held accountable to do, there's no fair comparison.

There's no way a sports athlete will fail to prepare for game day. It's just not going to happen. They're certainly not going to throw up their arms and say, "Guess what coach, I don't feel like practice today, in fact, I've been there, done that—just leave me alone." They'd soon be released from their team, as the management staff knows somebody else is waiting, dying for their job.

But, for some reason, in sales, they allow it to happen.

One Last Thing, the Authentic Thing

A true sales professional doesn't wait. A true sales professional holds themselves accountable. They continue to learn.

They don't expect to be told what to do. They invest in themselves.

If you're not willing to do the hard work, if you're not ready to be disciplined and dedicated, it's going to be tough. Unfortunately, there's not going to be many that will step in to help you along the way. You must fend for yourself.

Become the best version of yourself. Hold yourself accountable, hold yourself to a higher standard, and worry about improving you.

Knowing yourself is the process of understanding you. What makes you tick? Knowing yourself brings you face-to-face with self-doubts and insecurities. Self-reflection allows you to take a serious look at just how well you're living your sales life.

Knowing yourself is a conscious effort; you must lead with intent and purpose. You must take this approach with your career. You must lead your sales career with intention, purpose, and authenticity.

Authenticity is a choice. It's not easy, but for sales professionals, this is the difference between just getting by and making it happen. Self-reflect for a moment, asking yourself what does it means to lead an authentic lifestyle? It's hard work. It's looking right into the mirror, asking tough questions and answering them. You're in charge of your own sales career.

What's your plan? What do you need to do and when will you get there? It is totally up to you! Now go open the door to your authentic self! Watch what happens to your sales career!

It Is Your Choice!

How much are you willing to commit to yourself and to your future? One of the things I did this year was to create a manifesto, a series of commitments to myself that I choose to live by on a daily basis. I encourage you to make your own. Here is mine:

A *Selling from the Heart* sales professional is a new class— genuine, authentic, the real deal, in touch with who they are and are brutally honest with themselves.

A *Selling from the Heart* sales professional wages a war and becomes a minister to their clients in a profession riddled with unscrupulous, fake and disingenuous sales reps.

A *Selling from the Heart* professional leads with the heart and not the wallet.

A *Selling from the Heart* sales professional brings the human approach to sales by making it about their clients and what's important to them.

A *Selling from the Heart* sales professional seeks first to be understood as they turn transactional sales opportunities into transformational experiences.

Writing Your Manifesto

I'm not going to tell you there's a right or wrong way to write a manifesto; the style is completely up to you. You may want to make it simple, straightforward and state with passion why you believe in each principle.

Write down your beliefs, motives and the intentions around each of the topics. Your manifesto is an opportunity for you to lay it all out there by being real, genuine and staying true to YOU. Lay all the cards out on the business table for everyone to see and absorb. If you would like more help in writing your manifesto, then make sure your download The *Selling from the Heart* Self-Reflection Journal at www.sellingfromtheheart.net/journal.

I want to close with this. I believe in you, now it is time for you to believe in yourself. It is time for you to take your sales career to the next level. You owe it to yourself. Make the choice, and I guarantee you'll never regret it.

Selling from the Heart is a sales lifestyle!

I leave you all with this famous poem by Robert Frost.

The Road Not Taken

Two roads diverged in a yellow wood,
And sorry I could not travel both
And be one traveler, long I stood
And looked down one as far as I could
To where it bent in the undergrowth;
Then took the other, as just as fair,
And having perhaps the better claim,
Because it was grassy and wanted wear;
Though as for that the passing there
Had worn them really about the same,
And both that morning equally lay
In leaves no step had trodden black.
Oh, I kept the first for another day!
Yet knowing how way leads on to way,
I doubted if I should ever come back.
I shall be telling this with a sigh
Somewhere ages and ages hence:
Two roads diverged in a wood, and I—
I took the one less traveled by,
And that has made all the difference.
The road you decide to take will make a difference!

Signing off,

—Larry Levine

Praise for Larry

April 28, 2015 is the day Larry Levine and I became LinkedIn connections. I was two months into my entrepreneurial journey starting a disruptive talent acquisition/recruiting company called SomethingNew. What has transpired over the course of the past three-plus years has been an amazing friendship and admiration for what Larry has done for me. I have watched in in awe at what he has also done for so many others.

Larry began our relationship by jumping on calls with me to get to know each other as we both pursued our entrepreneurial dreams. Larry's support, without looking for anything in return, was inspiring. He recommended me to be a guest on several podcasts that he had been on. Despite all the success he had achieved in his career, he was always asking questions, thirsty for feedback and opinions even if those opinions differed from his own.

As two extremely transparent and opinionated entrepreneurs, we don't agree at times, but the respect I have for Larry is always 100 percent. Larry is exactly the same as he was over three years ago when we first met. His support is unwavering, and I covet his advice and insights.

Sunday morning is a time that I always look forward to, because I know it will start with a steaming cup of dark roast and a classic Larry Levine blog. His consistency in sharing his insight has been impressive, but it's the insight itself that blows me away. Every week his blog is pure gold and is something I don't think many people can match in terms of consistency and quality. Through these blogs, I have laughed out loud at his accurate depiction of sales situations and his analogies of "empty suits" and "commission breath" sales reps.

Larry's *Selling from the Heart* podcast has also had a tremendous impact on me. I have had the honor of being a guest and a fan. Larry and his co-host Darrell Amy have fantastic chemistry, and they always get the most out of all their guests which have included legends like Tom Hopkins.

Personally, professionally, in a blog, a podcast, a LinkedIn post or now in his sure-fire best-selling book, *Selling from the Heart*, Larry Levine is 100 percent authentic. His passion for teaching and giving is remarkable. His ability to strip away confusing industry jargon and acronyms leaves whoever is consuming his content with a crystal-clear idea of his message. Having had the chance to read advanced versions of *Selling from the Heart* has been an honor. His writing is clear, powerful and actionable. I'm excited to buy copies for friends and clients. It's an important work constructed with a servant's heart from a great friend and someone who simply gets it.

This is a book to break out your highlighter, take notes, dog-ear pages and refer to often. I hope you enjoy *Selling from the Heart* as much as I did!

Scott MacGregor, founder and CEO of
Something New and author of *Standing O!*

WANT TO SELL FROM THE HEART?

RESOURCES
Podcast
Subscribe to the Selling From the Heart podcast on YouTube or on your favorite podcast platform for weekly episodes that will inspire you to sell with authenticity and build trust. (www.sellingfromthe-heartpodcast.com)

Blog
Visit the Selling From the Heart blog to get innovative ideas to discover how your authentic self sells you. (www.sellingfromtheheart.net/blog)

App
Download the Selling From the Heart app in the Apple or Google app store to get instant access to resources to help you grow as a sales professional or leader.

INDIVIDUALS
Community
Find a community of like-hearted sales professionals in the Selling From the Heart INSIDERS group. (www.sellingfromtheheart.net/insiders)

Courses

Develop your skills with live and online courses that can help you apply the principles of Selling From the Heart to every aspect of the sales process.

Coaching

Get the support from a mentor as you discover your core purpose and break through to the next level in your sales career.

SALES TEAMS

Evaluation

Discover your team's strengths and development areas to form a plan to grow sales. (sellingfromtheheart.net/evaluation)

Training

Grow sales by developing your team's ability to build trust in every stage of the sales process including prospecting, selling, and client management. (sellingfromtheheart.net/trainging)

Leadership Development

Develop a high-performance sales team with sales leadership from the heart that creates and nurtures an authentic sales culture. (sellingfromtheheart.net/leadership)

CONNECT WITH US

www.linkedin.com/in/sellingfromtheheart
https://www.facebook.com/sellfromheart
https://www.youtube.com/@SellingFromtheHeart
https://www.instagram.com/sellingfromtheheart

About the Author

Larry Levine is the best-selling author of *Selling from the Heart* and the co-host of the *Selling from the Heart* Podcast.

With thirty years of in-the-field sales experience within the B2B technology space, he knows what it takes to be a successful sales professional.

In a post trust sales world, Larry Levine helps sales teams leverage the power of authenticity to grow revenue, grow themselves and enhance the lives of their clients.

Larry has coached sales professionals across the world, from tenured reps to new millennials entering the salesforce. They all appreciate the practical, real, raw, relevant, relatable and "street–savvy" nature of his coaching. Larry is not shy when it comes to delivering his message.

Larry is leading a revolution and a movement of authenticity, integrity, and trust in the sales profession.

Larry believes people would rather do business with a sales professional who sells from the heart as opposed to a sales rep who is an empty suit.

A free ebook edition is available with the purchase of this book.

To claim your free ebook edition:

1. Visit MorganJamesBOGO.com
2. Sign your name CLEARLY in the space
3. Complete the form and submit a photo of the entire copyright page
4. You or your friend can download the ebook to your preferred device

A **FREE** ebook edition is available for you or a friend with the purchase of this print book.

CLEARLY SIGN YOUR NAME ABOVE

Instructions to claim your free ebook edition:
1. Visit MorganJamesBOGO.com
2. Sign your name CLEARLY in the space above
3. Complete the form and submit a photo of this entire page
4. You or your friend can download the ebook to your preferred device

Print & Digital Together Forever.

Snap a photo

Free ebook

Read anywhere